Victory Every Day

Poems, Prose, Songs & Photographs By

Meredith Clayton Beal

Treasureland Inspire Press
PO Box 2132
Inglewood, California 90305
USA

ISBN – 978-0-615-70704-4

Library of Congress Control Number 2012953774

10 9 8 7 6 5 4 3 2 1

Distributed by Treasureland Inspire Press
PO Box 2132
Inglewood, California 90305, USA
Phone: +1.512.537.2116
sales@treasurelandinspire.com

www.treasurelandinspire.com

From a photograph of a cloud formation I saw as I flew over Casablanca that reminded me of a caravan of camels, to a picture of a mountain of cabbage taken in the beautiful hills of northern Thailand, to a snapshot of mighty Diamond Head taken before entering for a concert, to a photo I took while pondering the beauty of the day as sunrise peaked from behind the mountains brightening the Cape Town sky ... these are some of the images and feelings from them that I wish to share in this collection.

I awakened just before dawn one morning so that I could catch a seashore sunrise and unexpectedly found a gorgeous full moon setting one Tunisian night. The sunrise later was even more glorious. They were sights I will remember forever that I had to memorialize.

I rose before sunrise at Toda Lake to greet morning with a prayer before gathering with the great bodhisattvas. Milestone years of my Buddhist practice are commemorated with a celebratory poem and a corresponding image.

Other special moments range from the serene scene as I gazed across the rolling hills and mountain peaks in the land of the Maasai to when I awakened from a soft slumber to behold the sublimity of Mount Kilaminjaro, to the many, many sunsets captured in moments of august majesty. I wonder what beauty I will see today.

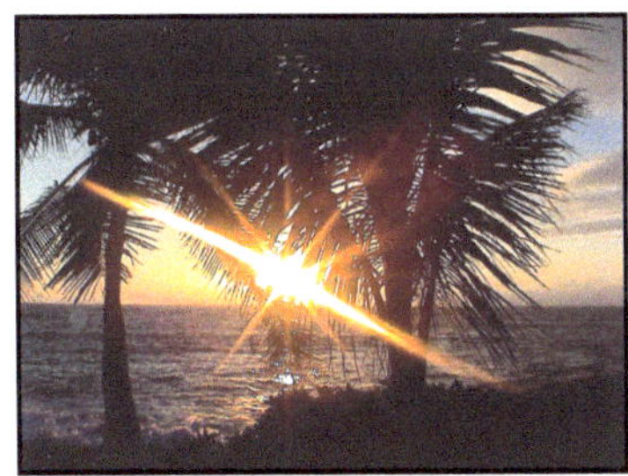

Cover Photo -- Hawaii

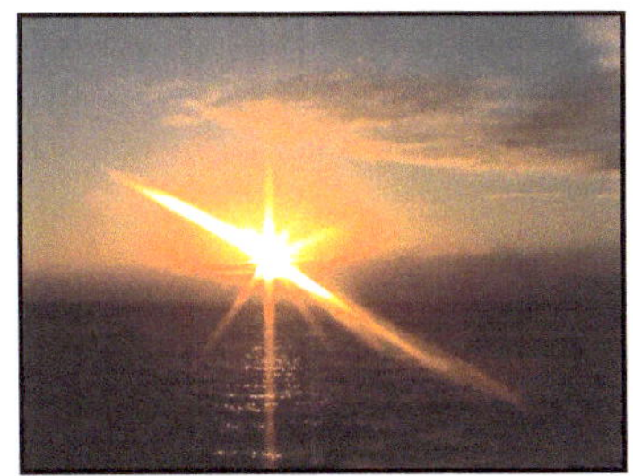

Back Cover Photo -- Malibu

DEDICATION

This book of poetic expressions, songs and photographs of life moments dear to me is dedicated to my parents -- my father, American hero and Congressional Medal of Honor recipient Marion Meredith Beal and my mother, the everloving Rohelia "Cherry" Beal, who raised me to seek the light, to endeavor to beautify wherever I am and to appreciate the magnificent wonders that life has to offer.

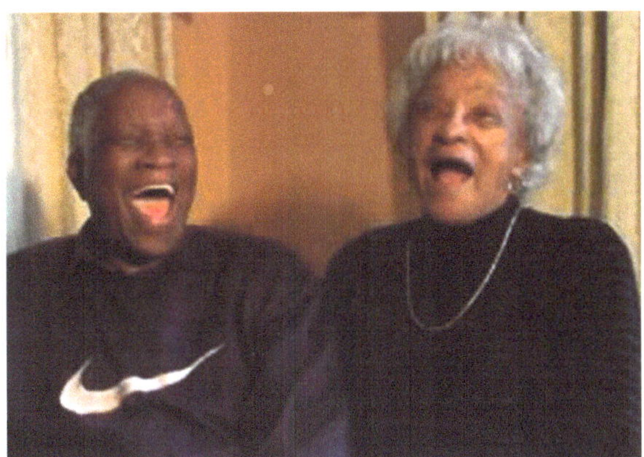

CONTENTS

Today I lived. That, in itself, is victory.

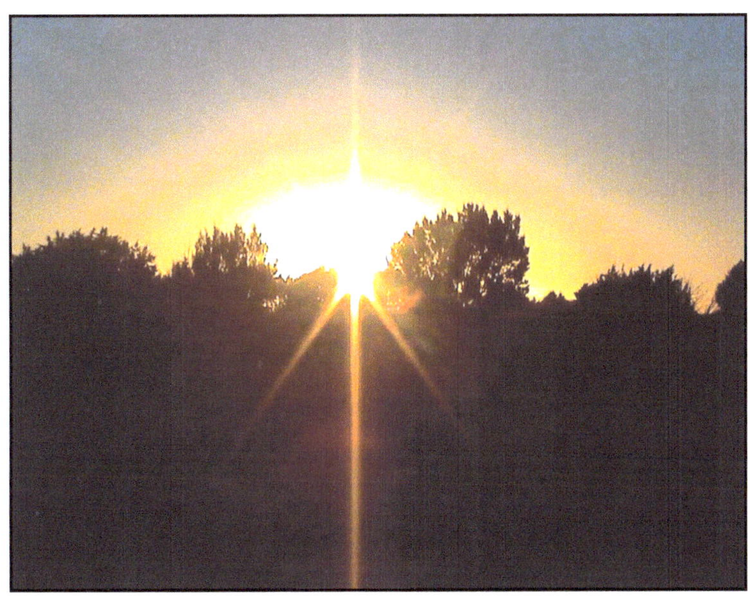

Victory Every Day

As the Sun rises each day
So do new challenges
So, too, emerges the power
To surmount each challenge
The vibrant, pulsing energy
Of joyful life awakens in my heart
And guides me to victory every day

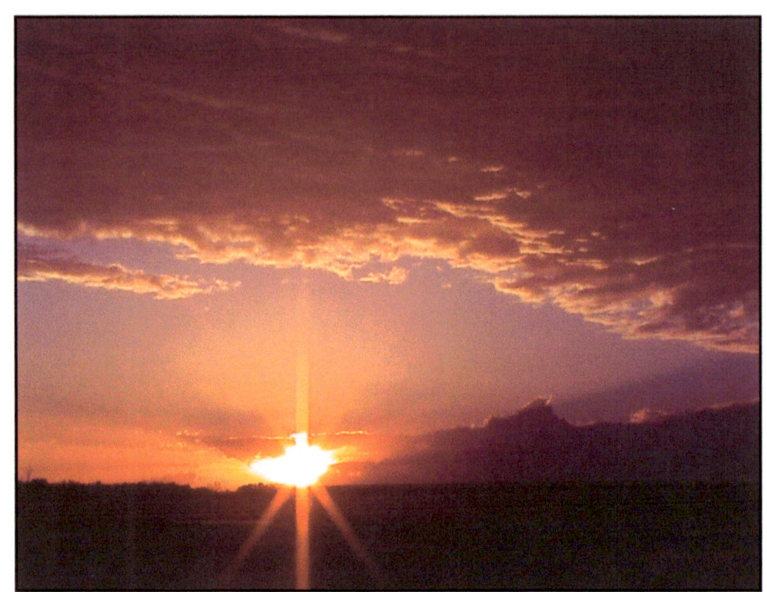

Hope

I am Hope ... hear me well
There's something very important I wish to tell
Though times be dark and full of fear
I am Hope and I am here
My name is Hope ... never should you fear
My everlasting presence forever dwelleth here
Though some say I've gone and others say I have died
My name is Hope and I am still alive
Always here am I ... and always am I near
Just think of me and suddenly I appear
I am with you always ... I never go away
My name is Hope and I am here to stay

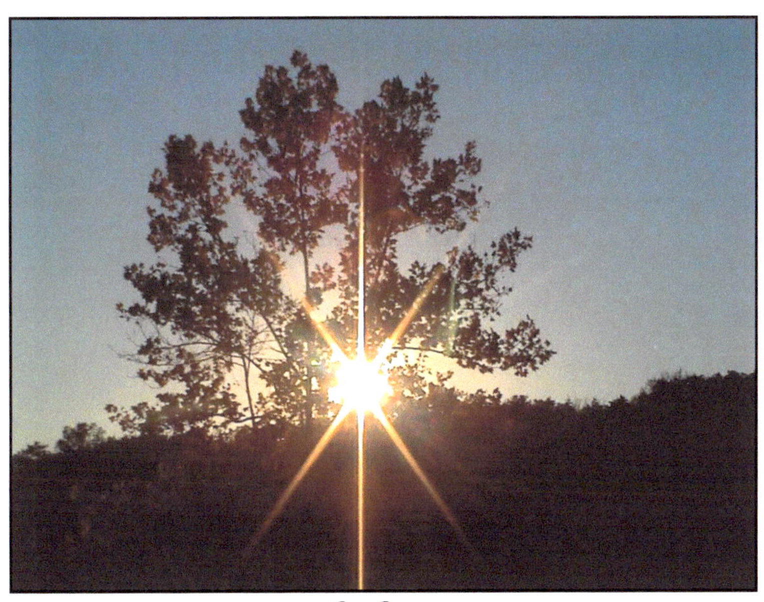

A Spark of Inspiration

All it takes is just a spark of inspiration
To reveal the brilliance of potential
Just a twinkle of an idea can open the door
To profound revelation and hence
Profound change
Just as a small spark can ignite a raging fire
So too can the impulse from a tiny seed of thought
Brighten the whole planet
A notion from a dream to be better
Can awaken a resolve to shine
Which in turn spurs an inkling of insight
That blossoms into an awesome awakening
A rich revelation
Just a gleam of light
Can be magnified into a shower of illumination
If …
There is inspiration

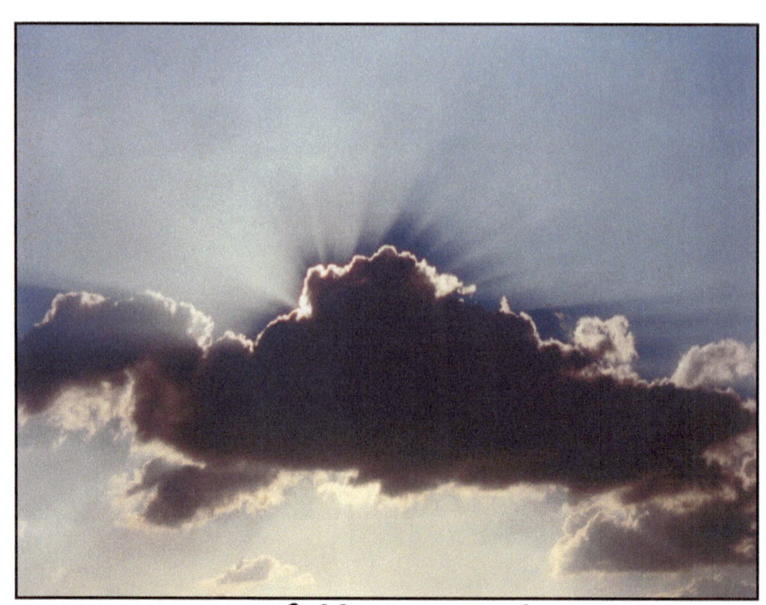

Hidden Potential

Though unseen ... it exists
Though unnoticed ... it is there
Though invisible ... it is real
Though hidden, the Sun still shines
No matter how dark the skies
Nor how dense the obscurity
How big the storm
How big the cloud
The Sun still shines
The Sun of Hope is everlasting
Blazing eternally from an unending source
And an inexhaustible reservoir of
Infinite potential
Though obscurred ... it exists
Though unrevealed ... it is there
Though unrecognized ... it is real

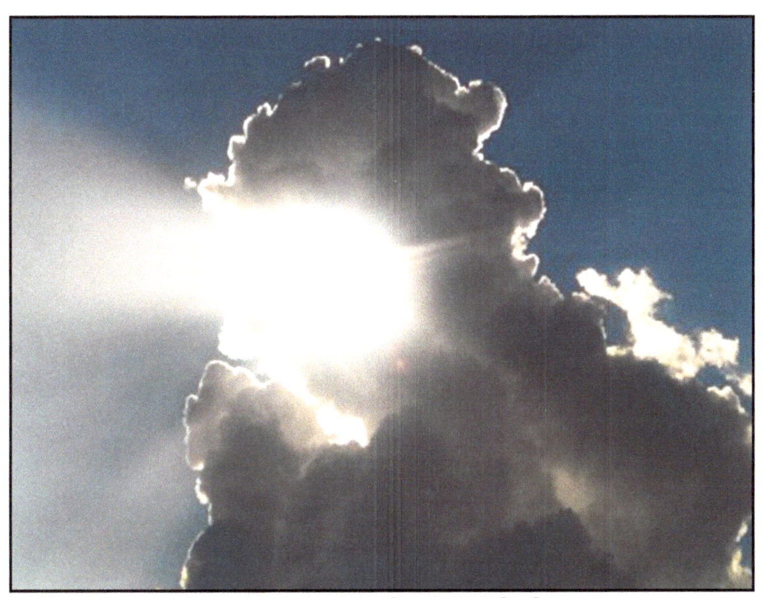

Potential Revealed

Just a hint of a notion of possibility
Gave rise to the thought of maybe
And just maybe with devotion and creativity
Gave shape to the idea of will be
And then will be with passion and tenacity
Transformed the once maybe into Is
Revealing hidden potential

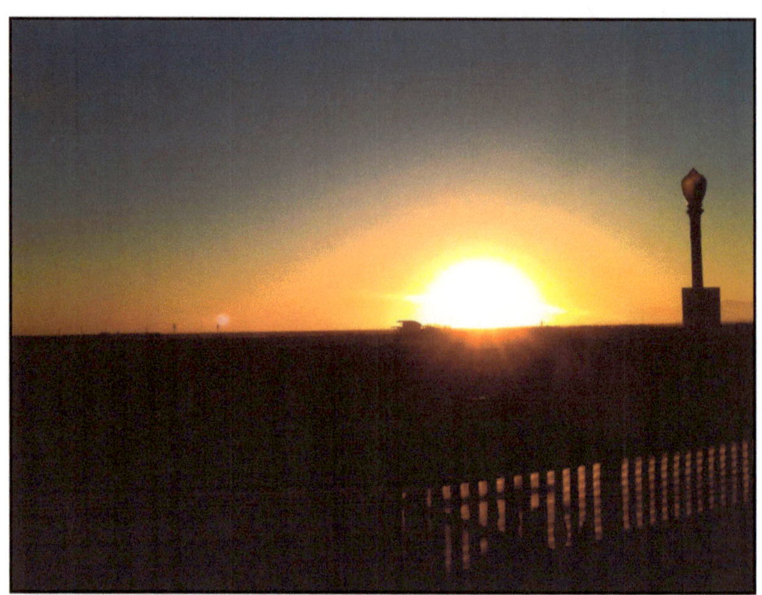

Seek the Light

It is not the reception of the known
But the process of the seek that is profoundly powerful
For when seek is supreme
No truth can remain unknown

Sunset

Sunset descends upon the land
Bearing violets among other hues
And smiling with its golden glowing brightness
Bidding farewell to another day

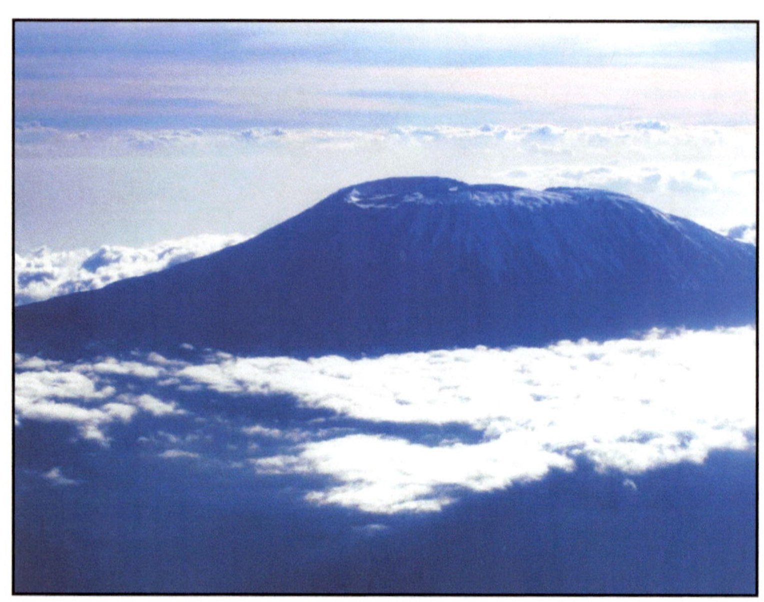

Majesty

Rising above the clouds in mighty majesty
The sacred mountain stands
A witness to uncountable human stories
And ever changing lands
Ascending above the clouds in royal nobility
The famed icon stands
In testimony to eons of ancient glory
A monument so grand
Thus you heard and thus you saw
More than any can remember
Serenely basking in the Sun
In all your royal splendor
Kilimanjaro … so you were named
So long, long ago
And still you are here
In a land without peer
Boldly standing tall
An entity of majesty
The highest peak of all

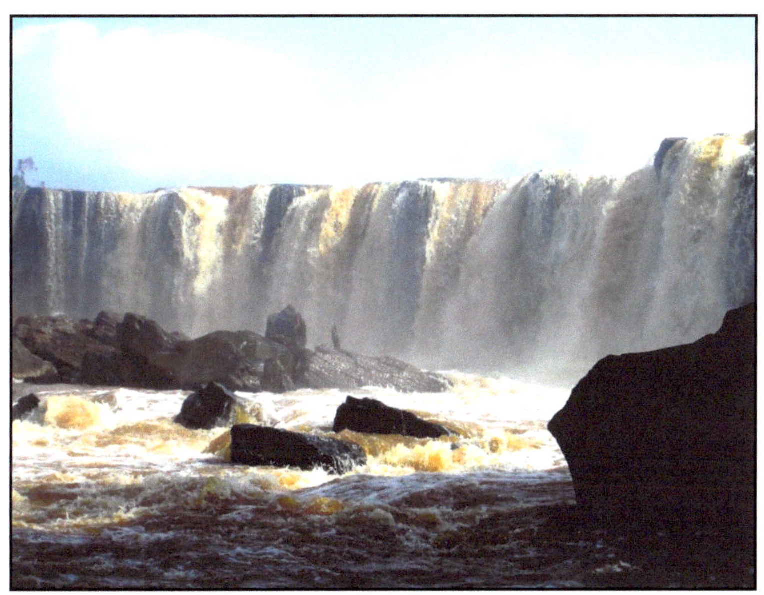

Nobility

The thundering roar of nobility resounds in the air
The roaring thunder of water reverberates everywhere
Surging with force gained as water flows
From land to land to land
Gaining in momentum from continuity
Moment to moment to moment
Swelling into a mighty display of nature's power
A vibrant current sweeps through the hills
Clarifying, purifying, refreshing all in its path
As it accumulates, aggregates and culminates into
The great, powerful waterfall thundering in nobility

Thika , Kenya

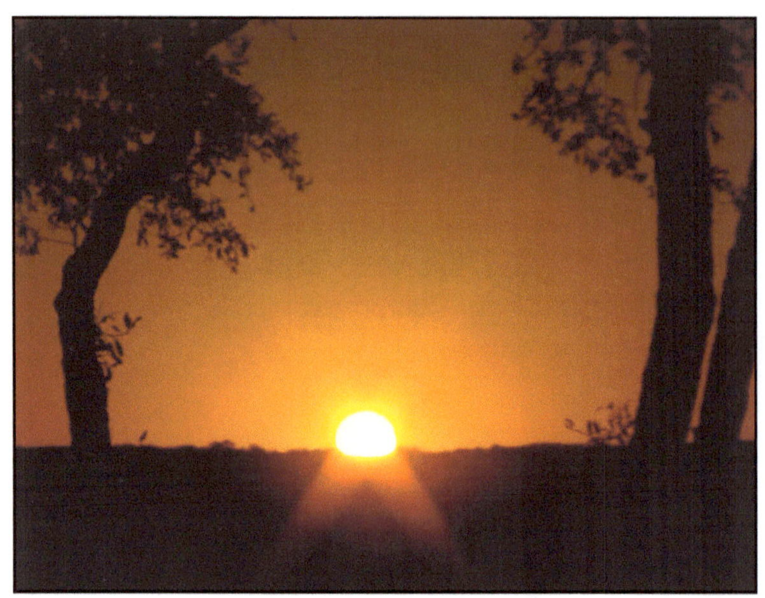

Beauty of the Morning

Morning light
Serenity fills the air as day life slowly awakens
The symphony of nature begins
Birds sing their songs
Squirrels chatter their morning prayers
Water creatures echo their awakening in the rivers
Morning mist floats earthward
Becoming morning dew
Pale violet skies transform into rich warm orange
As the sun peeks over the horizon
Morning is here signaling the end of night
Darkness fades to light as the Sun rises
Dawn -- a new day
Sunrise
It's dawn
Behold the beauty of the morning

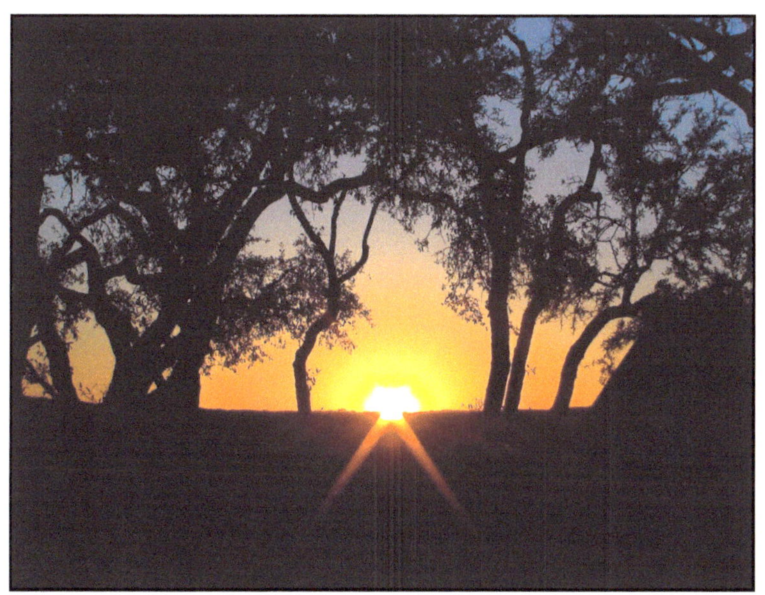

The Light of Dusk

Look to the horizon as the Sun sets
And watch the changing sky usher in the twilight
Brilliant blues morph into deep purple shades
As the Sun sets in the western sky

A simple reward for a day's work well done
To see the light of dusk on the way home
Illuminating the road for just a short while longer
As the day comes to an end

Last light of the day, one more look at the setting Sun
One more peek before slipping behind the horizon
One last peek ... oh but I must
Get one more glimpse of the light of dusk

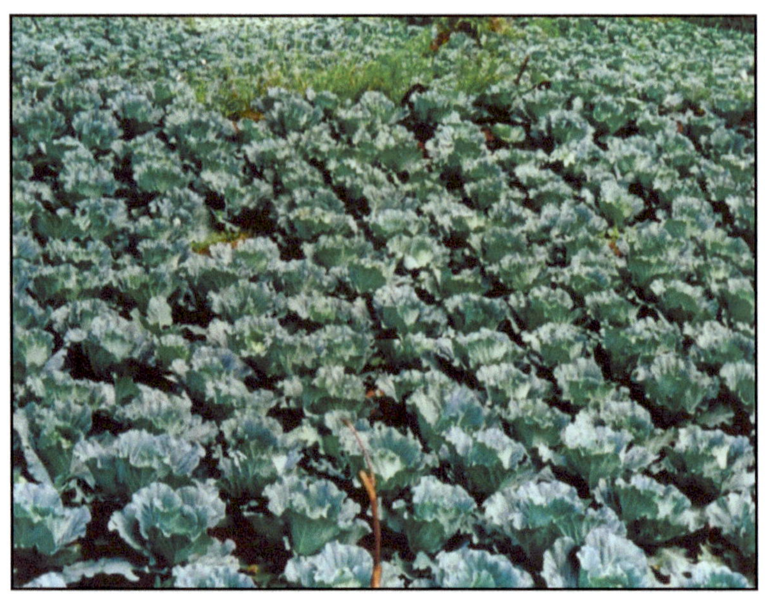

Abundance

The command of abundance thundered throughout the land
And the Earth complied in prolific splendor
Exuding prosperity and overflowing with sufficiency
A planet abound in plenty
A bountiful harvest awaits
May all earthlings partake in the
The thrill of abundance

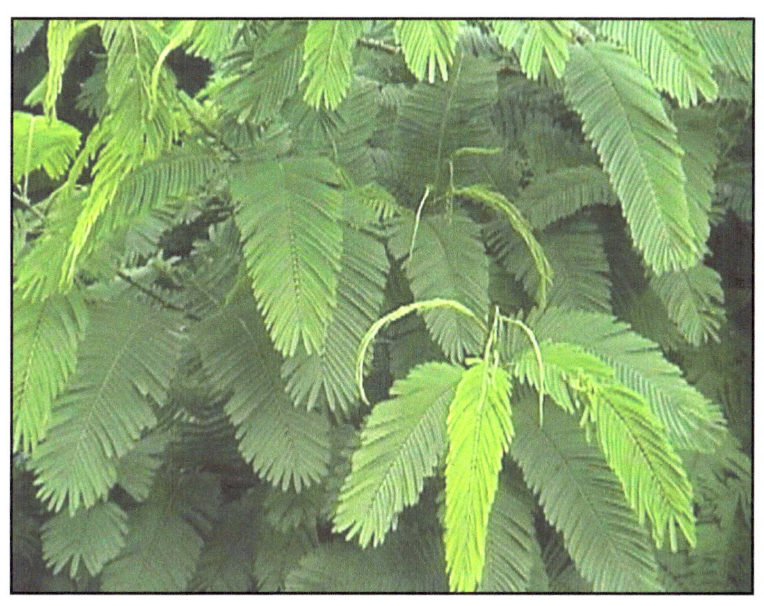

The Green Life

Ah, but for the green life
What would life be
Or would Earth life even be
The green life performs its magic
Turning sunlight into energy for living
For all that walks the Earth, flies the skies and swims the seas
The mystic transformation of chlorophyll
Into fuel for life
Without the green there would be no life here
Embrace the beauty and juvenation of
All shades of the green life
Coloring the world as flora everywere
Fulfill their glorious role as nature's alchemists
Transforming light into life
Transforming the golden glow of the Sun into
Vibrant, vivid, living green
I sing praises , prayers and appreciation
To the green life

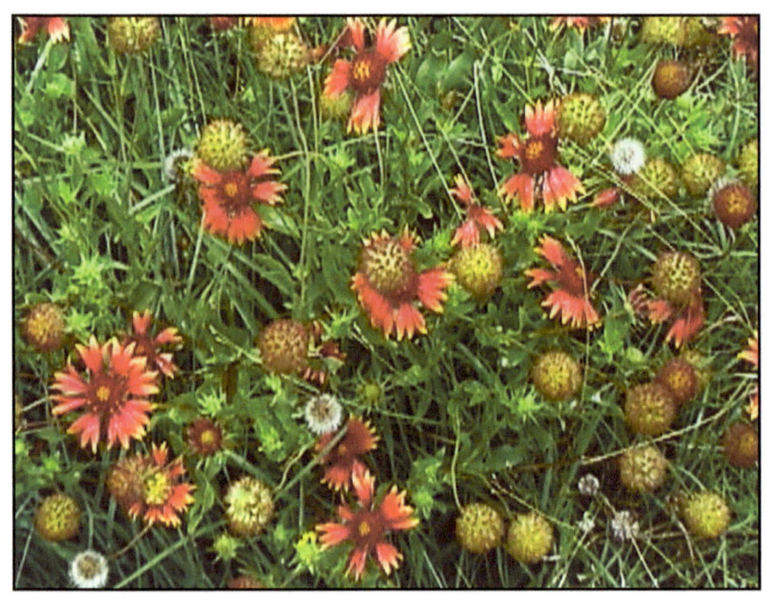

Flower Dance

Sunshine nourishment and rain
How could we ever ask for more
Dancing with joy at the coming of spring
The time we've been longing for
Stems and stalks sway with the wind
In rhythm morning 'til night
Blossoms reaching skyward for the Sun
With their leaves clapping in delight
Harmonic melodic harmonious melodious
The sounds of nature in bloom
Rhythmic enrichment choreographic fulfillment
Flora dancing to the lively tune
Indian paint, poppy, lilac, daisy and daffodil
Bluebonnet, gardenia and tulip and many many more still
Carnations, roses, gladiolus ... and birds of paradise
All join in a great garden party of life
In celebration of nature's spring song
All seeking the beauty of Earth to enhance
Come together to partake in the great flower dance

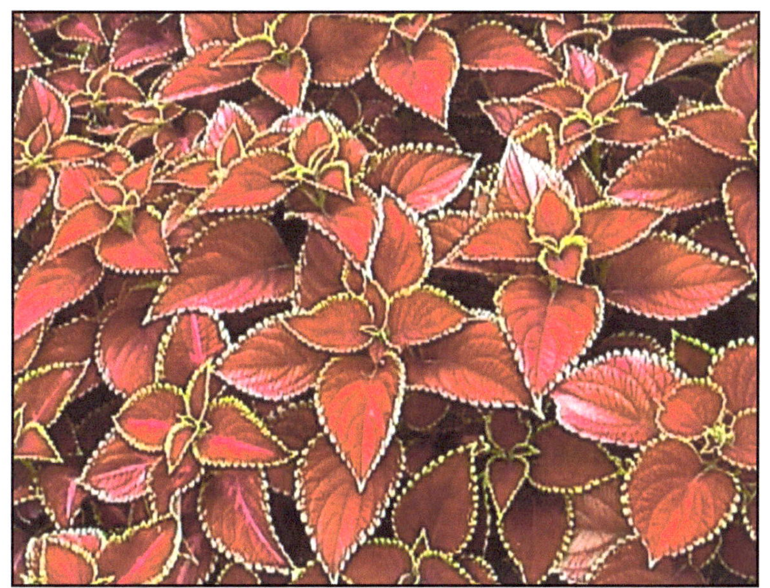

Symmetry

The architecture of Nature seeks perfect design
Searching for the most efficient use of space
Creating beauty through simplicity even in the complex
Drawing shapes that inspire wonder and amazement
Painting with a palate of infinite color
Directing light to reveal the vibrant vibrations
Orchestrated by the artfull flow
Such order, such balance, such alignment
All done with masterful symmetry

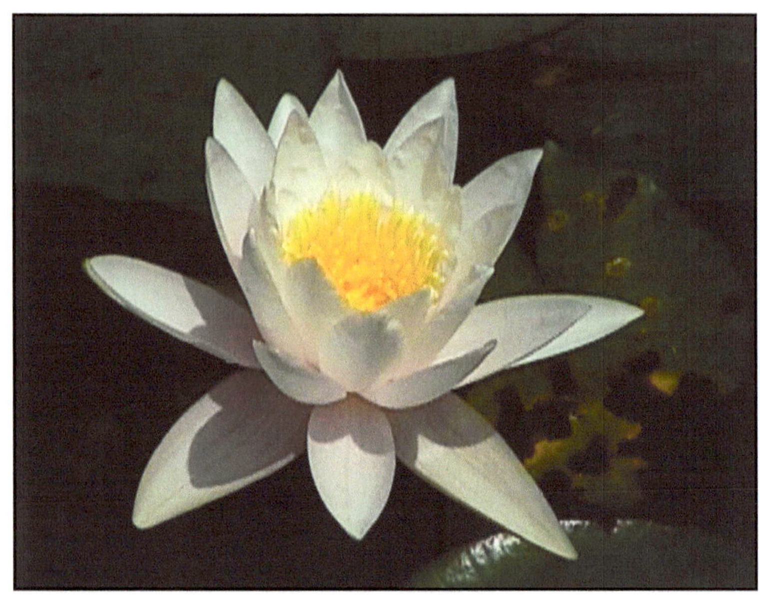

Seed and Blossom

Was it seed then blossom
Or blossom then seed
Was it the chicken or was it the egg
Which came first ... the age old question
That has forever perplexed humankind

The bewildering dichotomy may be caused by
The notion that one must have come before the other
Which may not necessarily be so
Could they have emerged together
Has the inherent potential for seed and blossom always been
And the reason and result emerged at once
Since they depend upon each other to exist

As mystic and intriguing as
Why the Sun rises in the east
And sets in the west
Is the mystery of seed and blossom

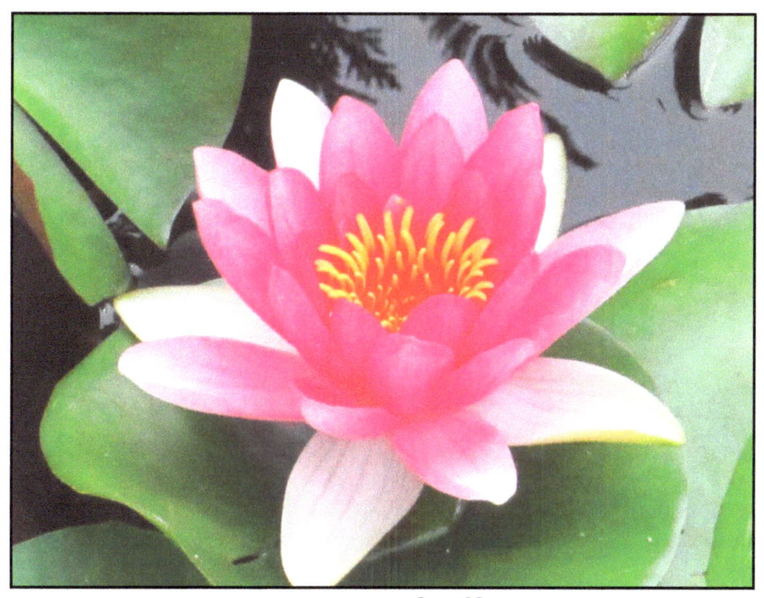

Cause and Effect

What effect can there be without cause
What result could ever unfold without reason
For the unbroken chain of causality
Links the past to the present and the present to the future
What I am now and what I do now
Reveal all three
There is a law of causes and a law of effects
But far more profound and enabling
Is the law with the mysterious nature of
Simultaneous cause and effect
The essence of destiny
The instant causes are made effects exist
Therein lies the power of the present moment
I can make the perfect cause now
To create the perfect destiny and the effect will exist now
And the future will reflect that reality
Ah, how glorious ... Ah, how victorious
How wonderous is the law of destiny and how wonderous indeed
Is planting the seed of simultaneous cause and effect

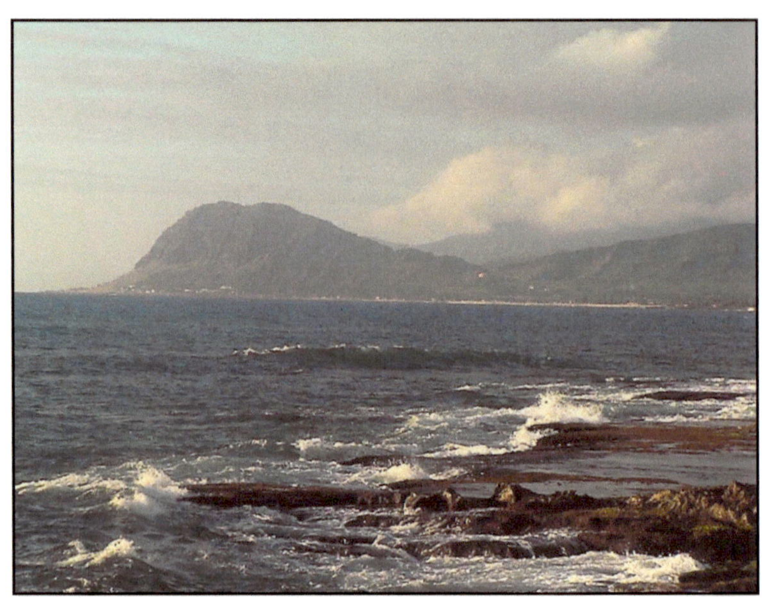

Ebb and Flow

Ebb and flow
The tides come and go
And the winds of change
Never cease

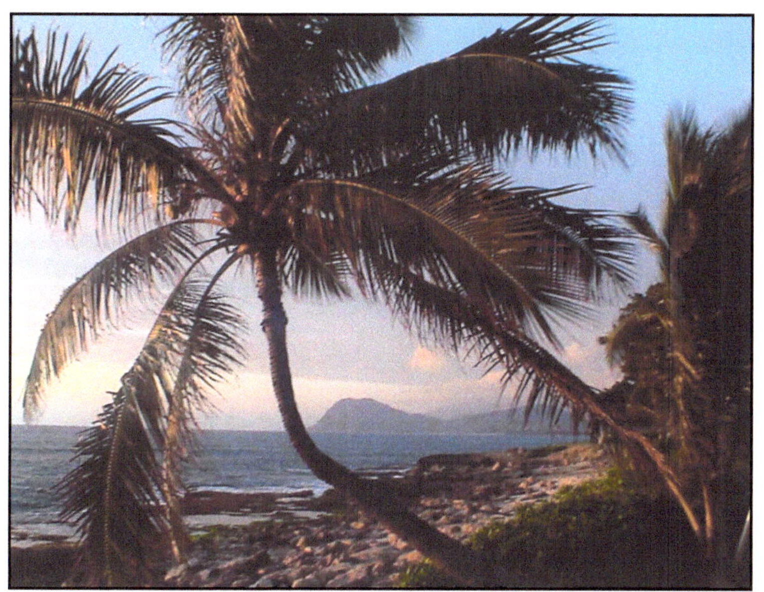

Adventure

Through the door of dreams
And the window of imagination
Unlimited possibilities unfold
Adventure awaits the seeking spirit

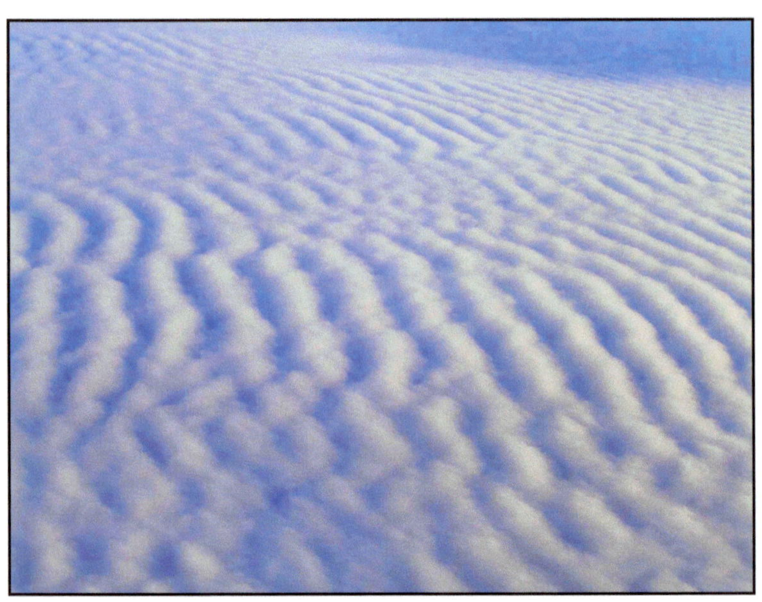

Field of Clouds

Was it birds that plowed
The fields of clouds
To sow the seeds of rain

Did the eagles fly
Supremely high
Seeking beauty, good and gain

To create the field
Of fruitful yield
Producing boundless benefit

That blossoms forth
With living force
And bounty preeminent

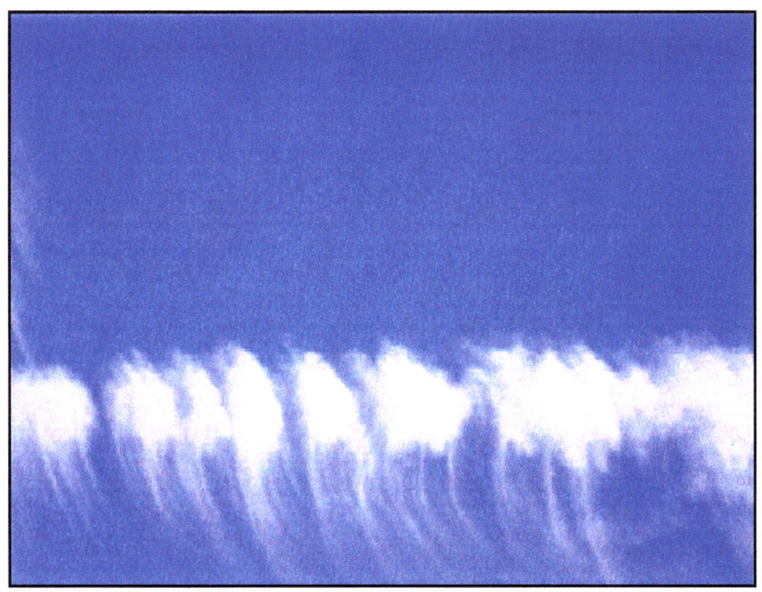

Camel Walk

Marching through the sky, aloft in the wind
A caravan on high, the journey begins
Cross desert sands, the merchants they talk
Sharing mystic stories of the skyborne camel walk
"Good change is a-comin', see the camels," they cried
And soon winds of fortune brought better times by

The procession sails on over land after land
Witnessing untold tales of the creature called Man
Cross ocean waves, the sailors they talk
Sharing magical tales of the skyborne camel walk
"Good change is a-comin', see the camels," they said
As the sailors dreamed of better times ahead

From days gone by and ages of old
The caravan continues its leisurely stroll
Cross mountain peaks, the travelers they talk
Sharing whimsical legends of the skyborne camel walk
"Good change is a-comin' see the camels," they cheered
"It's an omen that much better days are near"

Circling the Earth again and again heralding the coming of fortunate winds
Merchants, sailors and travelers all say look to the clouds to show you the way

Whenever you see that curious trail in the air
There's a reason to smile and jubilation to share
For when Camel Walk appears in the sky
Good change is a-comin' they all testify

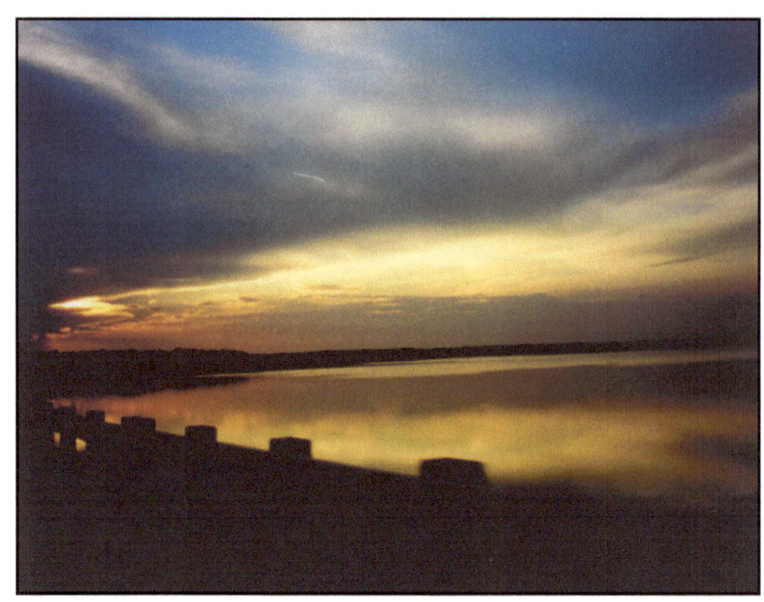

Tranquility

A *feeling of ease and calm comes over me*
As I ponder the joy of the day
A sensation of peace and quiet embraces me
As I savor the flavor of life
Tranquility ... tranquility ... tranquility

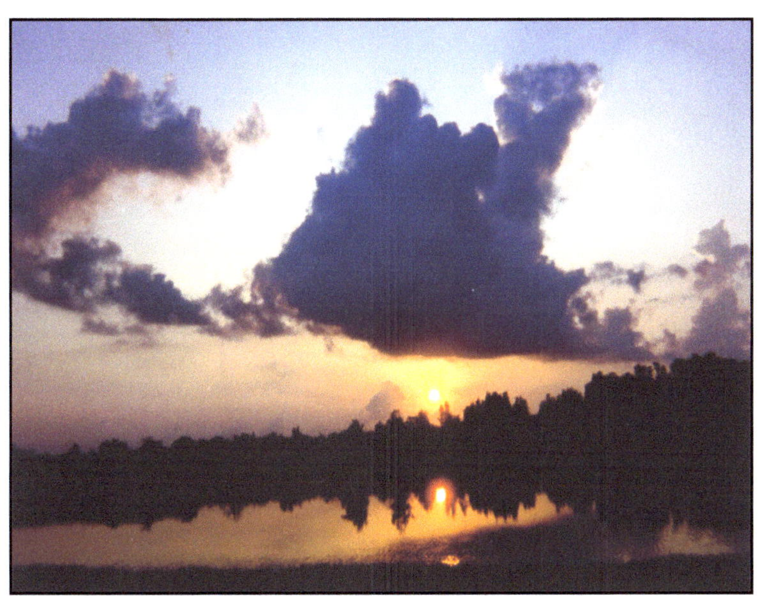

Sunrise at Toda Lake

Greeting sunrise at Toda Lake
To commune with the morning Sun
And revel in the blessings of Myoho
In a land adorned with precious gems of legends of old
The mighty Bodhisattvas of the Earth
They came from far and wide
A cluster of human gems
Another gathering of friends of Myoho
On a quest together
To invigorate the world
With infinite hope for the future
To reaffirm To reinvigor To rededicate
To the glorious mission they share
Sunrise at Toda Lake
A time of peaceful repose
Morning prayers with the coming of dawn
Reflecting on the victories and dreams
That are part of the evolving story
Of kosen rufu of the land

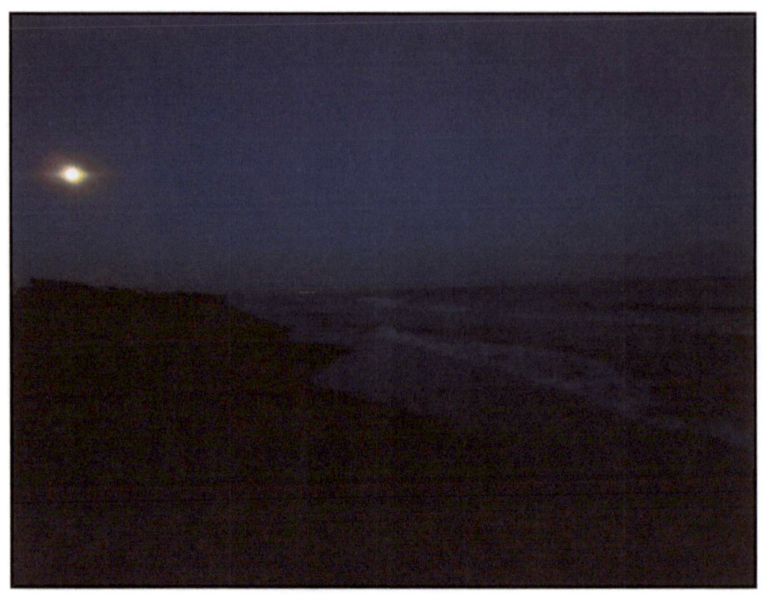

Night in Tunisia

My first night in Tunisia I arose just before dawn
To catch a seashore sunrise
And to my surprise right before my eyes
A bright silver moon brightened the sky
Lounging in the sand listening to Dizzy and Bird
Taking me on a nocturnal journey through melodies so cool
While ocean waves played a rhythm so smooth
One Tunisian night
And what a night and what a sight
The moon gets closer to the western horizon
As the glow of impending sunrise grows in the eastern sky
Now I'm listening to Chaka sing about "A long time ago in the forties"
While I await moonset and sunrise
Amidst the still quiet of Mediterranean calm
And now it's Bird and Miles playing the legendary tune
And my mind wanders to back in the day
Watching the masters live on stage
Taking us to new heights in the musicsphere
Ah, to see moonset and sunrise at the same time
To see such a glorious sight while embracing glorious sound
Is a blessing indeed
To behold such a scene so serene
One Tunisian night
... And the melody still lingers on

Serenity of a Full Moon

It was a quiet night
With a gentle breeze tickling the leaves
As night birds sang an evening song
It was a peaceful eve
With a lovely breeze caressing the trees
As nightfall croons an evening song

Peeking through the trees a tiny glimpse of light
Striving to make itself seen
And as the world turned the light became brighter
Revealing a sight to be seen

Suddenly breaking through the clouds
Beaming with tranquility
A bright and full October moon
Shining with serenity

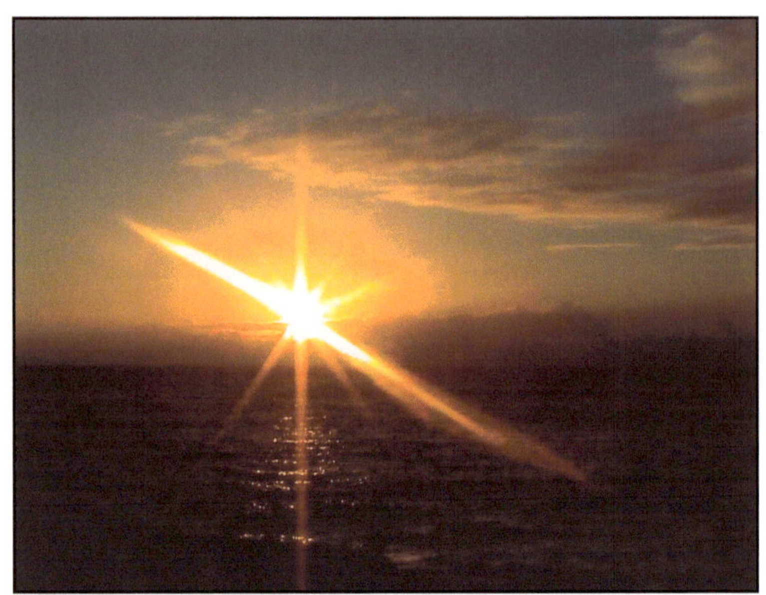

A Time Called Now

The forward eternity we call
The future
The backward eternity we call
The past
All are lived in a time called
Now
It doesn't matter where you live
Nor when
Only how

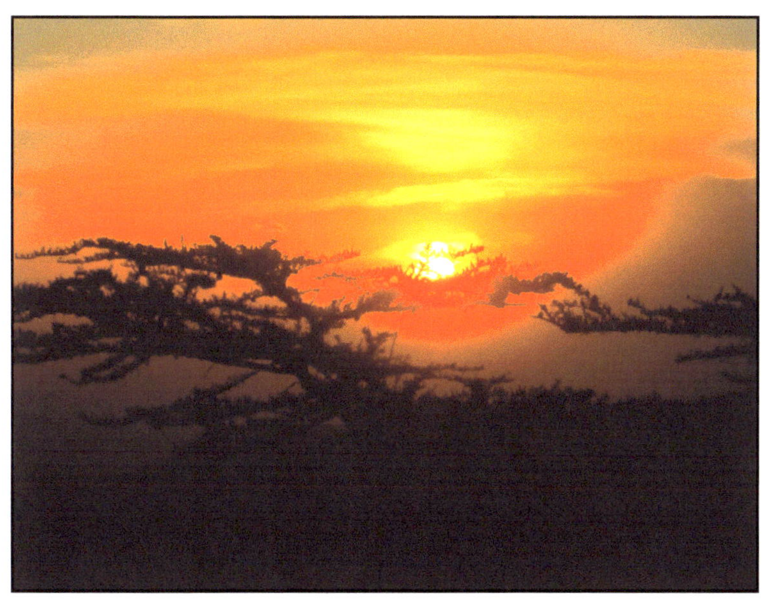

Africa Rising

Pulsing with the vibrancy of original human life
A nurturing mother to all
Sleeping giant awakening in the dawn
Oh, Africa rising

Brewing in the depths of ancient human experience
A reservoir of wisdom for all
An ailing planet awaits your merciful morn
Oh, Africa rising
Rising, rising, rising
Africa rising
Rising to give new life to the world

Simmering with hope for a brighter future to see
Tomorrow becomes today
Sleeping giant awake at Millenium Dawn
Oh, Africa rising
Rising, rising, rising
Africa rising
Rising to give new life to the world

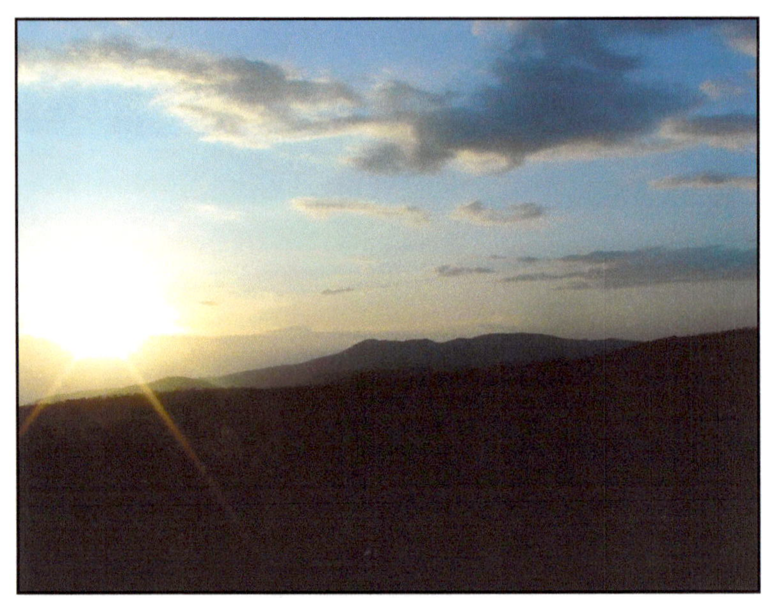

Ever Shining

We see light of the Sun every day
And never does it say
I just don't feel like shining today
Like the Sun
Ever shine Ever shine Ever shine

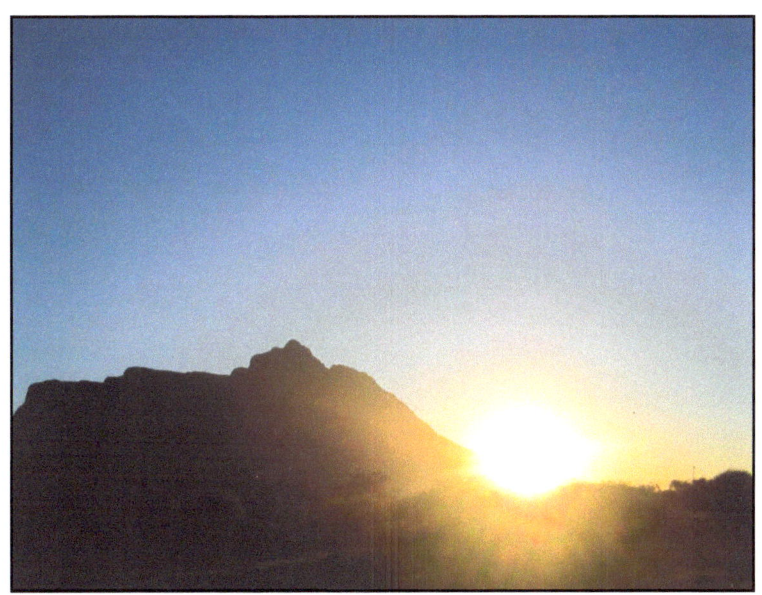

Even Brighter

Wiser kinder happier more inspired more imaginative more insightful crispier fresher healthier more caring more compassionate more cheerful better brighter braver more fortunate more focused more futuristic stronger smarter sharper more thoughtful more loving more respectful friendlier faster fitter more vigilant more vigorous more energetic more efficient, more effective more creative more caring more courageous more friendly, more helpful more courteous more productive more humorous more reverent more fun more fearless more humble more joyful more jubilant more human. May this year be even brighter

From Meredith's 2012 New Year's Greeting

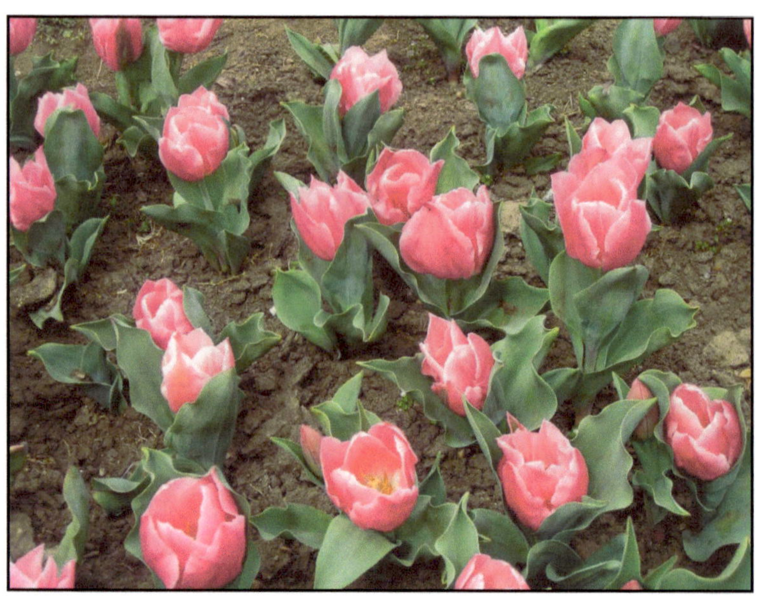

Let Us Pray

Let every heart feel the comfort of a warless world
Allow the Earth to glow in the warmth of harmony and peace
Among all the peoples in all the lands
Let the wounds of centuries of hatred be healed
May outbreaks of civility erupt all over the planet
Let us pray

From the song "Arms Down" by Meredith Clayton Beal

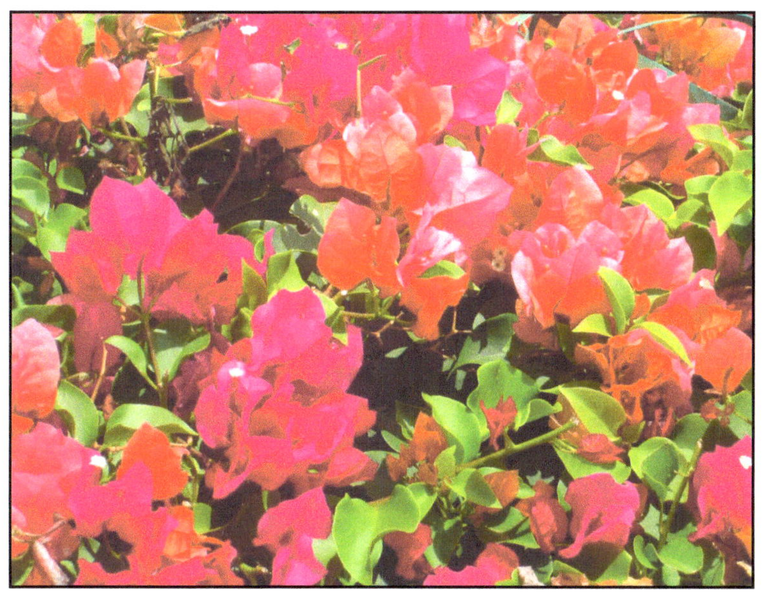

Happiness

Can you see harmony in place See a smile on every face
Hear laughter ever ring Hear humanity all join to sing
Happiness oh yeah, happiness, yeah yeah
Happiness oh yeah
Everybody longs for happiness

Can you see harmony in force
When everybody taps that ever loving source
Feel compassion all around
Hear the sound of human joy resound
Happiness oh yeah, happiness, yeah yeah
Happiness oh yeah
Everybody deserves happiness

From the song "Happiness, Yes, Yes, Yes" by Meredith Clayton Beal

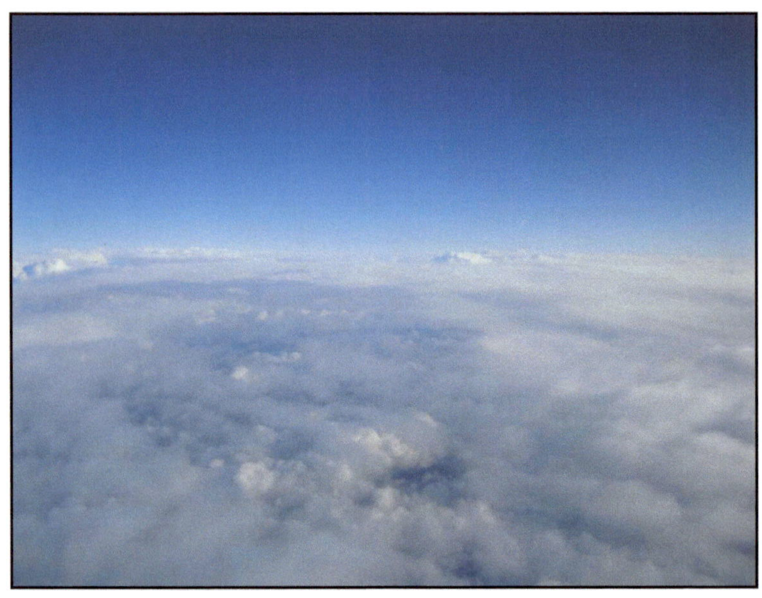

The Pilot's Seat

Kneel each dawn at the pilot's seat to guide your life in the right direction
And each evening sees you kneel once again to straighten the course even more
Day after day hears your voice resound
Over and over so pure and clear
You know your fortune's waiting there
Treasure tower for all to share
Start each day from the pilot's seat to raise your life condition higher and higher
An invocation for this life so divine to emerge the most beautiful self
Each of us Captains of the Universe leading lives as models for all
For the proof is how We live what We do and what We give
To this life ... for this life
Face the Sun each dawn from the pilot's seat
Watching kosen rufu slowly make its way
And even if the dusk finds you standing all alone
Still you have the spirit to carry the mission on
Day after day hears your voice resound
Over and over so pure and clear
You know your fortune's waiting there
Treasure towers for all to share

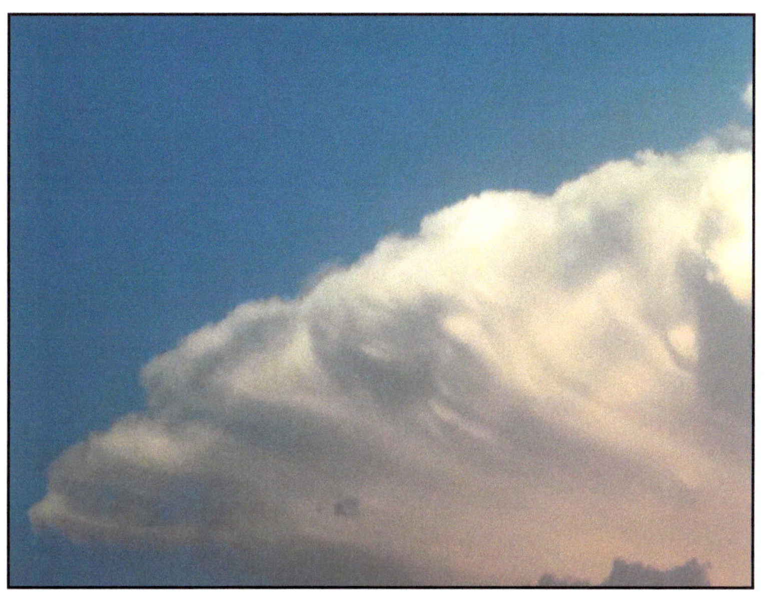

Island in the Sky

Like an island glistening in an open sea
On a blanket of blue
A cherished haven for a weary sailor
A welcomed sight to behold
After many long nights at sea
Take a journey on a cloud of imagination
On an island in the sky

On the island in the sky is a mountain
A mountain there just to be climbed
Ascending the slope with wonder
Seeking a most magnificent view
From the peak
Of the mountain
A mountain on an island in the sky

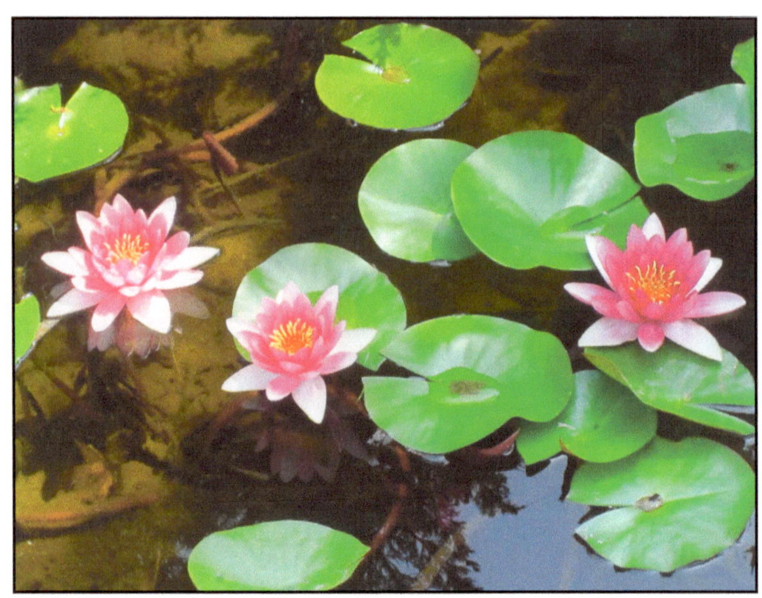

My Three Mentors

Three envoys of the Mystic Law
Arrived in the land
To pave the way for peace
In the footsteps of the master mentor
They marched through the land
A message of happiness to teach
Vowing to repay a debt of gratitude
Deeply immersed in beatitude
In unity and continuity
A trinity leaving a grand legacy
Bodhisattvas of the Mystic Law
Appeared in the land
Advancing the cause of peace
Gathering ever greater multitudes
They walked through the land
With the message of happiness for each
Leading by example they boldly showed the way
Living lives of value each and every day
My three mentors etched in history
The formula for total victory

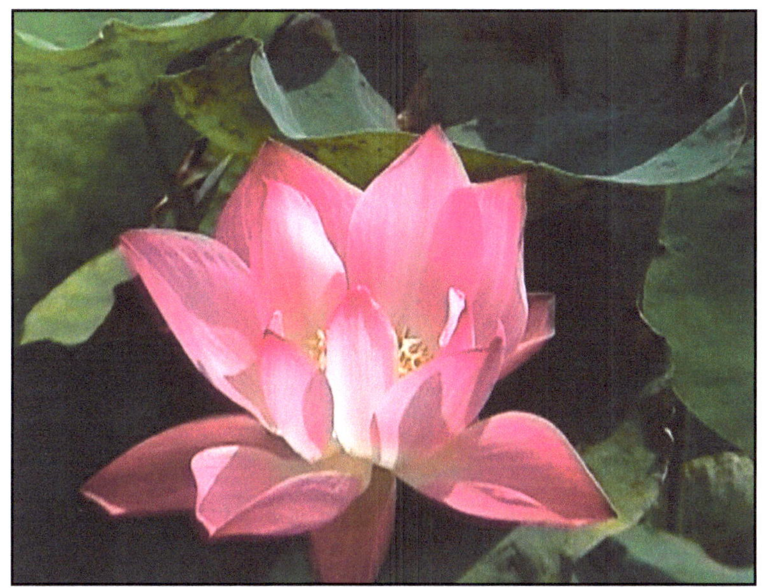

Year Thirty Five

So glad am I that I heard the Mystic Sound as my quest for true self began
Early on my journey in life I found, a principle on which I could stand
With the hands of many friends of faith, always perpetually there
With courage, compassion and a smile on our face, a glorious mission we share
Still on the path I've stayed year after year after year
Planting seeds of good fortune every day, and living a life full of cheer
Victories mount as the years go by, treasured moments that will long endure
For the better me I long to see, A winning life is assured
Blossoms of good fortune continue to sprout, 'cause I was taught how to nurture the seed
My three mentors blazing a trail without doubt, they taught the way to succeed
So wonderous it is that I survive, how fabulous it is that I'm alive
This is the year for me to thrive … I celebrate Year Thirty Five
I awaken in the morn to realize that I, once again, have another day to live
How wonderful, how marvelous, how magnificent … another opportunity to share the
Smile of loved ones, pleasant thoughts with friends or a nod of fraternity with a stranger
Another day to be enchanted by the curious shape of a cloud
Or intrigued by the melodious song of a bird
How many days left for planting? No one knows for sure ... just keep planting
The words of two of my elders continue to inspire me:
"I'm gonna wear out not rust out," said my great aunt, the legendary
Dr. Christine B. Cash, who lived to the age of 99; and
"Live with joy, treat people right and savor life," said my grandmother, the
legendary Big Mama Lucille Burrell, who recently passed at the vibrant age of 109!
Live joyfully and savor life. That's what I'm gonna do! One of the biggest benefits I've gained over 35
years of chanting Nam Myoho Renge Kyo is to be able to live joyfully
Day to day, despite whatever's going on
I'm going to savor life... I'm going to thrive
I'm going to joyfully celebrate
Year Thirty Five!

Essence

Forward is the motion
Mighty is the drive
Even is the countenance
Eternal vigor is alive
Keep the sight
Upon the mark
As you walk the sacred path
Take not lightly what you saw
For all that you witnessed were expressions of
The essence of the ever living law

Mystic Night

On a mystic night I ponder the meaning of my life
And contemplate my destiny the mission meant only for me
To be the me that I must be to truly fulfill my destiny

On a mystic night I wonder the duration of my life
How many days are left to see and just how long will my life be
Will all my talents be set free to truly fulfill my destiny

I have less than 20,000 days left to live ...
Tomorrow will be 19,999
I have an infinite amount of energy to give
But only so much time

On a mystic night I gaze over yonder
At the golden moon setting in the noctournal sky
Looking into the future I see the sight
With vision clear of a glorious life
Living everyday with all my might
And so I pondered ...
One mystic night

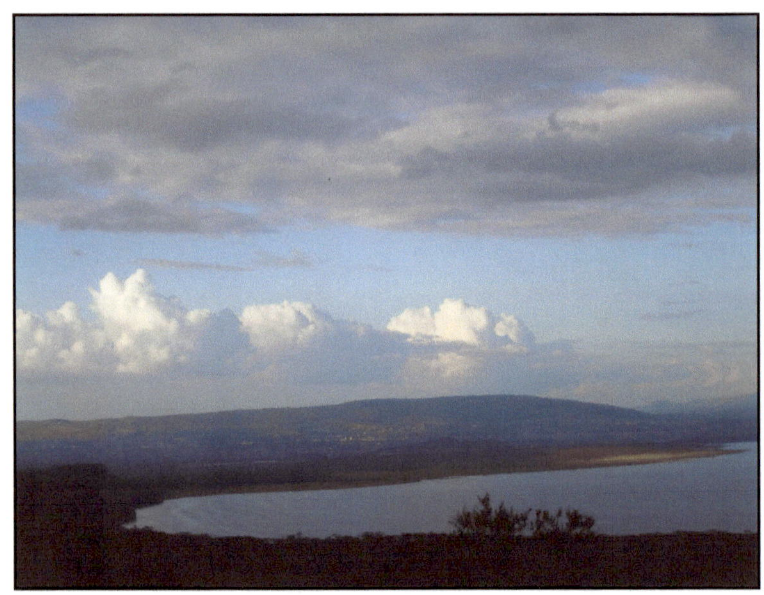

Peaceful Day

Serenely embracing the breathtaking mountain top view
Admiring the beauty of what nature has painted
On the canvas before me
I feel the peace of the soothing still of the lake
As birds and other fauna rest along its shores
Peaceful rolling hills echo the calm of the day
While white puffs of playful clouds dance in the distance
Riding the winds toward tomorrw
Oh, the serenity of a peaceful day

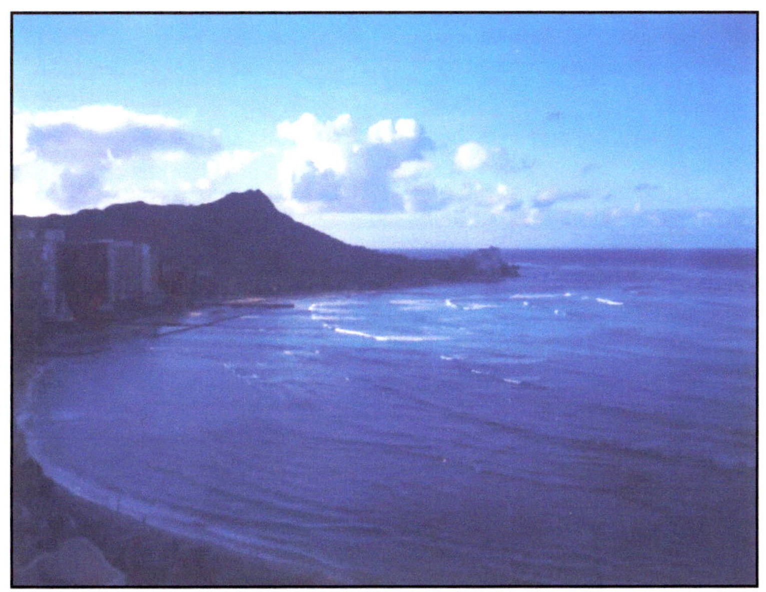

The Diamond Blue

They came from star systems galore from all over the Universe
To make their way to a gathering place located on planet Earth
There's this spot there they say where you just have to be
'Cause there's an assembly of extreme musicality
The most moving, soothing music you'll hear
Permeating the entire atmosphere

Sitting for two hundred millenia and more the most famous crater around
Tonight you're the scene of a concert supreme with the most glorious of sounds
Glittering like a blue diamond ... reflecting in the Pacific sea
Shimmering in the gentle winds ... the breezes of Waikiki
A venue so grand and stately you see, majestic, yes it's true
They call you Le ahi ... Diamond Head ... tonight I'll call you Diamond Blue

They entered the cone of the mystic volcano to hear the masters play their tunes
Herbie and Wayne sending waves of song, skyward from Club Diamond Blue
Famous, even in galaxies afar, the most marvelous, wonderful sounds
Coming from within the volcanic cone at the grandest party around

Crowned by a night of sound extraordinaire they returned to their various clans
Carrying the rhythms of Earth music to all those distant lands
To share with beings everywhere with testimony so true
Of the joy of the vibrant vibrations
A night of Jazz at Diamond Blue

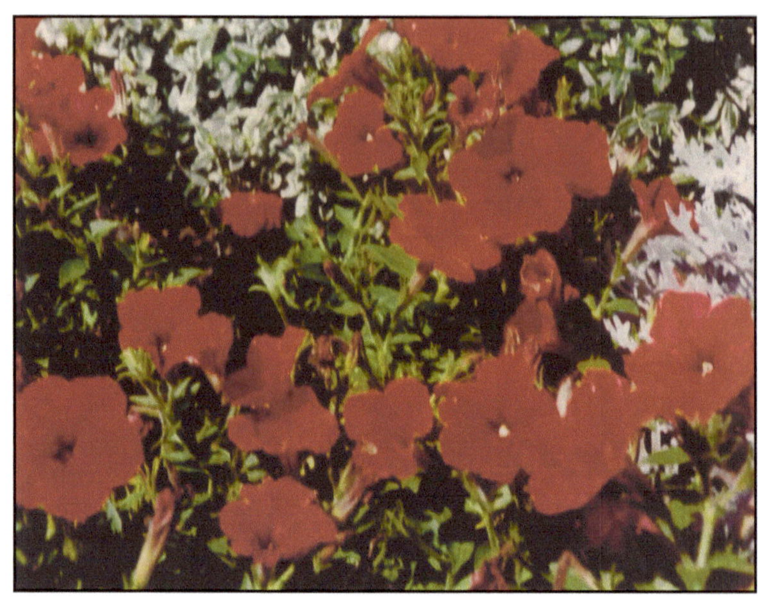

Passion Flower

I saw love from the start
Blooming in your heart
Like a daisy
You drive me crazy
Passion flower ... passion flower
It is now that I suppose
That your love is like a rose
In the springtime
The way you touch my heart
So tender
You're gentle as an evening breeze
And mellow as the evening seas
You know I love you
Let me touch you
Passion flower ... my passion flower

From the song "Passion Flower" by Meredith Clayton Beal

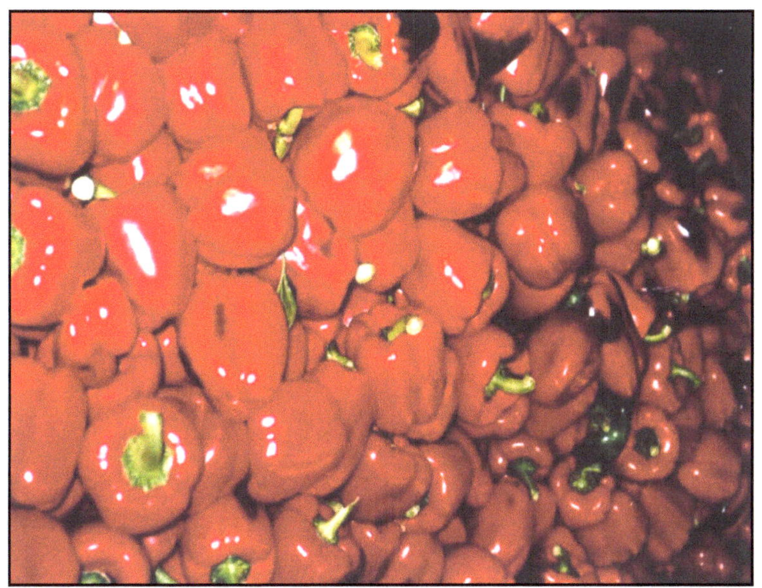

The Harvest

The long awaited time to reap the fruits of labor
To see the result of toil and sweat ... patience and sacrifice
Will the efforts pay off ... will the time spent be worthwhile
These questions have been asked by
Generation after generation as people everywhere
Endeavored to survive ... endeavored to sustain
Endeavored to grow ... endeavored to prosper
Will the seed planted now live ... will it mature
Will it blossom ... will it bear fruit
These questions are the basis of the anxiety
That people the world over have experienced throughout history
And the energy of that anxiety provides the basis for
The elation, the relief, the satisfaction and the appreciation
That bursts forth at harvest time
Share in the joy of The Harvest

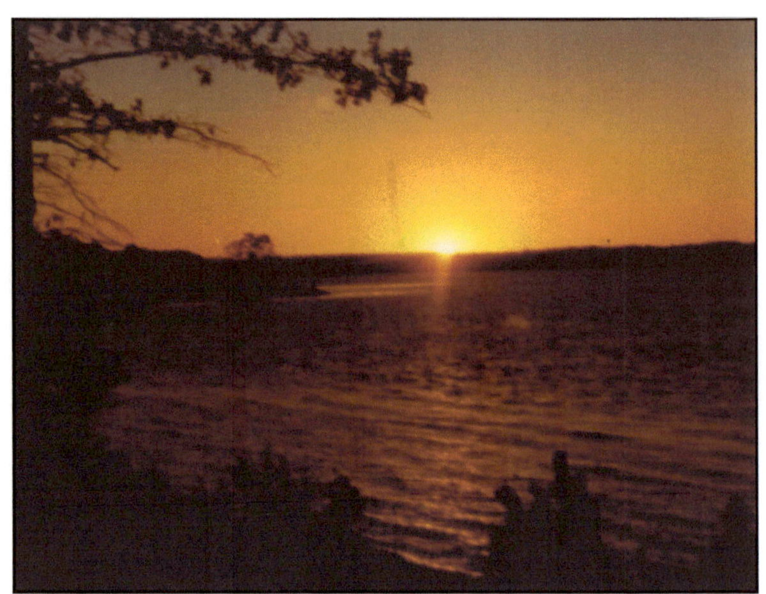

Daydreams

Daydreams
Just the visions in our minds
Of the lives we've longed
So very long
To lead

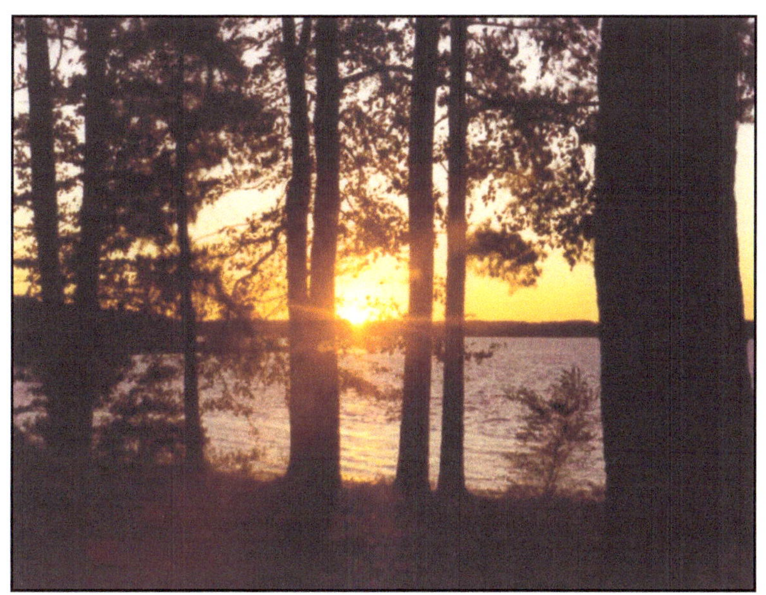

Remember

The times when I am distressed
Are the times when I forget who I am —
A sublime human being dwelling in the earthlands.
When I am discouraged, I need only remember
who I am

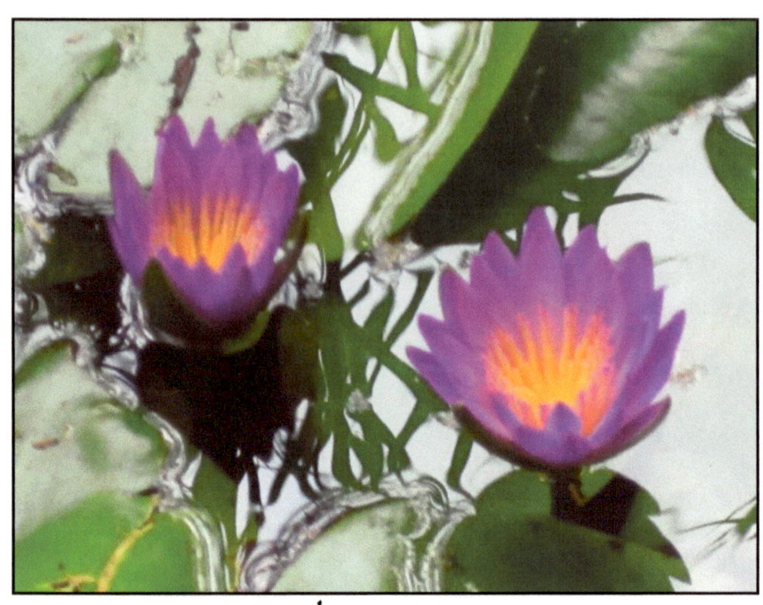

Twenty Years

Twenty years -- first score
Embark upon the journey through the next door
Practice and practice for decades more
To gain the crowning glory of the virtues four

Decade three -- second round
A higher life condition to be found
Again and again invoke the Mystic Sound
To bring forth a life of joy profound

Ten years times two -- a perfect score
Higher and higher like an eagle I soar
Millions and millions of daimoku I sing
As the sound of happiness rings and rings

Nam Myoho Renge Kyo

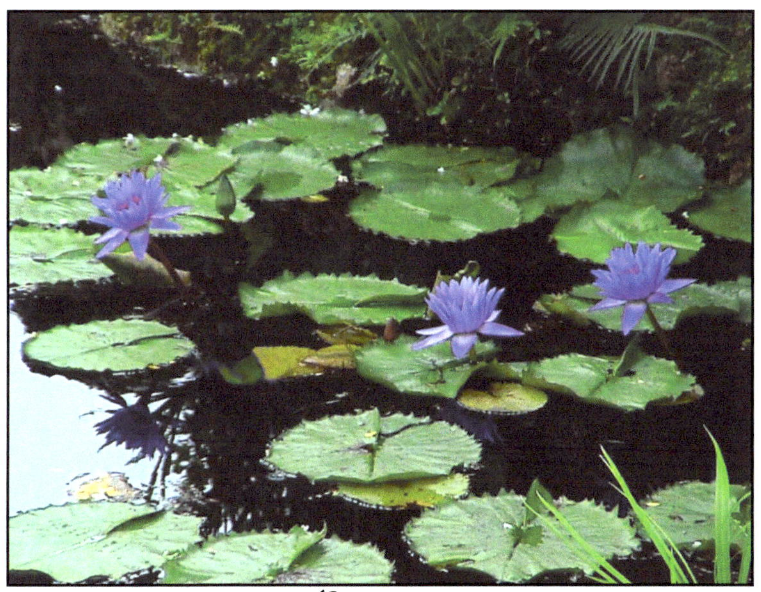

Thirty Years

How can life be more pleasurable than to be showered with benefit immeasurable
How can one sing a more joyful song than the beautiful ballad of life prolonged
What treasures would one offer to live just one more day ... How could I ever pay for my
Ten thousand days ... How many joyful times have I seen since -- I cannot count
How intense have those joys been -- I cannot measure ... What infinite treasure
Uncountable, immeasurable, unfathomable I say
I behold the value of thirty years today

Twenty thousand gongyos done Twenty million daimoku sung
Eighty four thousand battles won As I savor the taste of life
Character building day by day Wisdom growing as I pray and pray
For absolute happiness to stay and stay I see the wonder of thirty years today

I utter the sacred mantra beckoning the emergence of abundant wisdom
And summoning the appearance of absolute freedom Endless solutions for my
Human revolution ... rhythm refined ... perfect life designed
I gaze in the mirror at my true self to fathom the infinite universe inside
And grasp the eternity of the moment The full embrace of life amid the certainty of death
What good fortune to live and be able to make the highest cause and receive the highest
Effect ... to live a happy life and die a happy death
Living the dream of profound elation secured by daily value creation
Crowned with supreme appreciation ... three decades living the Golden Way
I celebrate thirty years today

Nam Myoho Renge Kyo

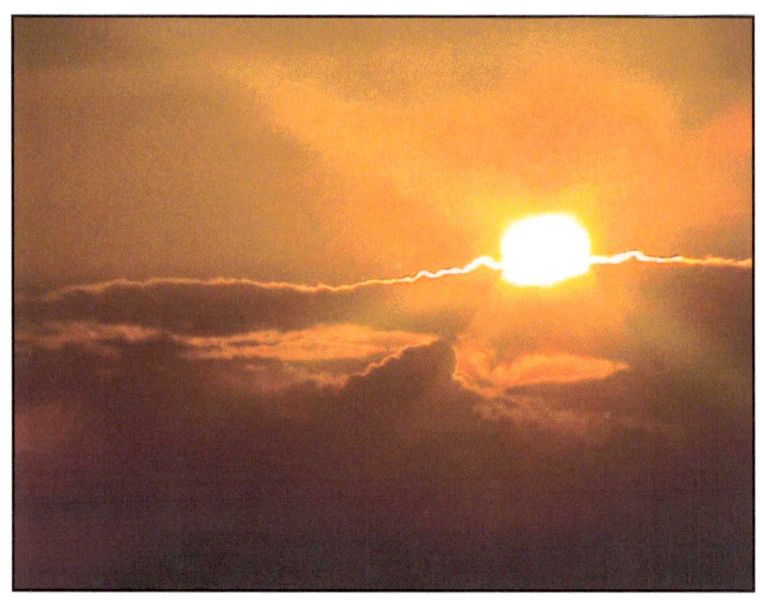

Loving Rays

Beaming down on me
Shining for all to see
Never losing their way
Ah, those loving rays

Never ceasing for a moment
Round-the-clock flowing current
Glowing day after day
Behold the loving rays
Causing growth on land and sea
Giving birth to flower and tree
Join the blades of grass as they pray
Embracing the ever loving rays

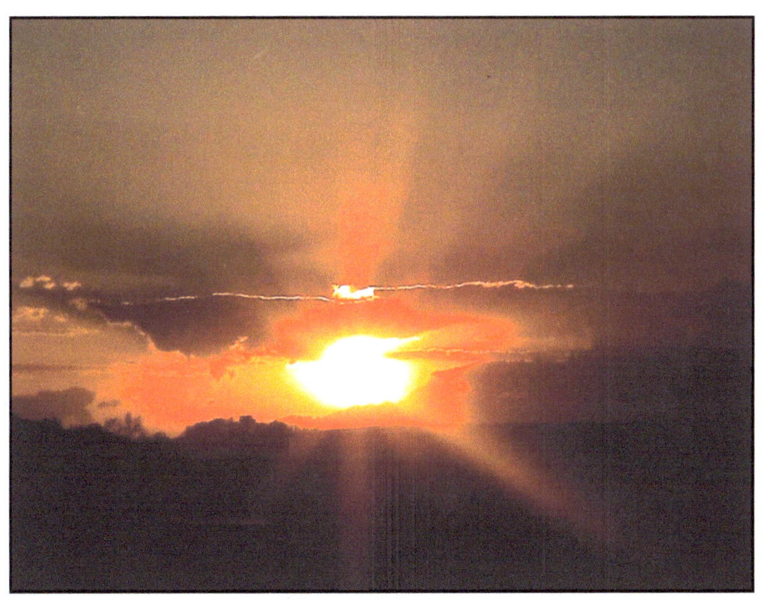

The Golden Days

We are living in the future
Of people of olden days
And too we're living in the past
Of humans in future time
In this vast collection of moments
Of which we call a lifetime
The most important moment is always now
For the past is only memory
And the future is just a dream
All that is real lies in now
We must cherish the joy now
We must live for the joy now
These are the golden days these are the treasured times
Don't let 'em slip away cherish the joyful times
These are the golden days these are the precious times
Don't let 'em slip away treasure the joy

From the song "The Golden Days" by Meredith Clayton Beal

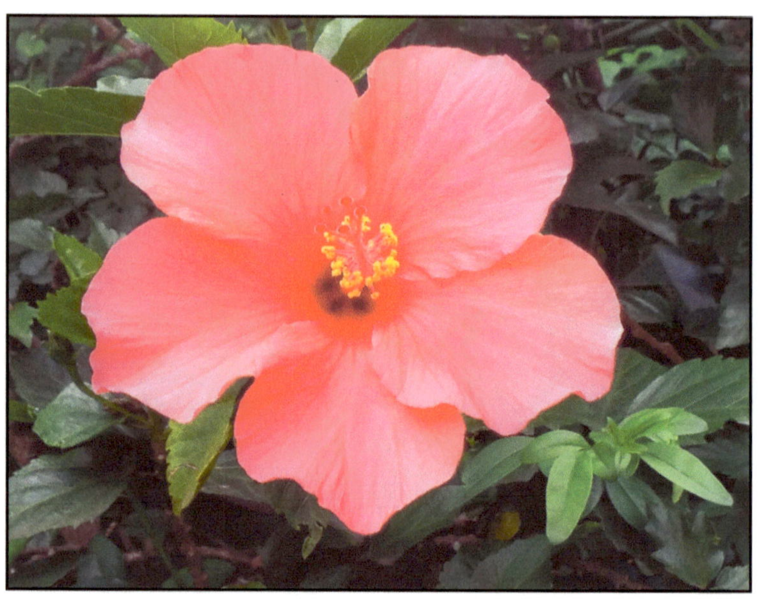

Just A Moment of Peace

Just a moment of peace is what we need
And all it takes to get started just to plant the seed
Blooming day by day we'll soon come to see
Lasting moments of peace
Just an instant of calm to clear the air
And once it gets started it can spread everywhere
Spreading land by land one and all can see
Lasting moments of peace
In times of conflict in the heat of hostility
When things just seem to go wrong
In times of discord and days of disharmony
When it seems we can't get along
Just take a moment, let's take a moment
Just take a moment, all it takes is a moment
Just take a moment, let's take a moment
Just a moment for peace

From the song "Just A Moment of Peace" by Meredith Clayton Beal

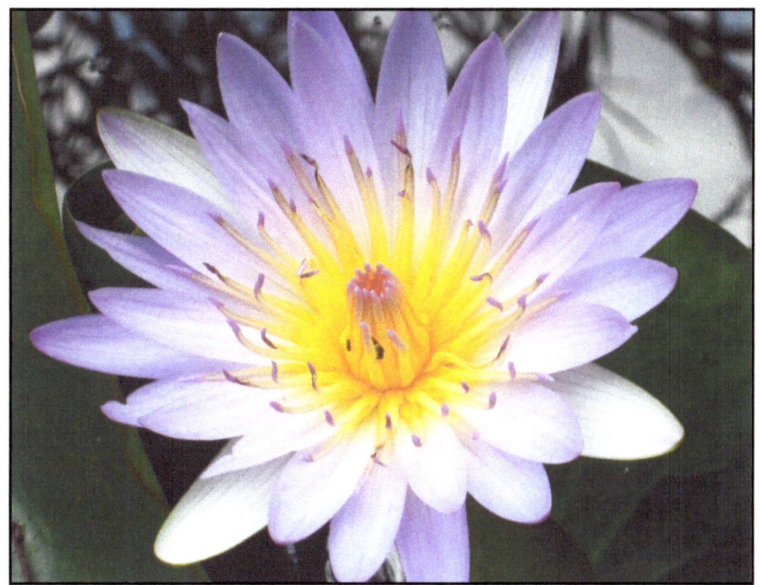

Invocation

Thank you Mayor Leffingwell. To the honorable Mayor, Council Members and citizens of Austin, on behalf of the Buddhist lay organization, SGI-USA, I wish to express our deep appreciation for this opportunity to invoke the law at this esteemed gathering.

As representatives of this noble City of Austin's people and stewards of its resources, you have a great responsibility. May you carry out those duties with pure hearts, clear minds and firm resolve to elevate the quality of life of all its inhabitants.

The Buddha spoke of the great, wise, compassionate, powerful life force that dwells within us all – innately inherent in everyone. May the Council's deliberations and decisions be guided by that great wisdom, insight and compassion and that they lead to the highest gross community happiness possible.

Nichiren Daishonin, the Buddha of Mappo, in teaching about unity, said "If the spirit of many in body but one in mind prevails among the people, they will achieve all of their goals whereas if one in body but different in mind, they can achieve nothing remarkable." It doesn't mean that we all have to think alike but if we can become one in mind around the common goal of creating the highest well being for the most people, then the synergy of that unity will produce remarkable results.

May you summon from within yourselves, the imagination, creativity and cooperation to find new ways to help more people and through your deliberations, may the vision emerge to navigate this fair city through the myriad challenges it faces now and in the future. Let us work and pray in harmony as we all strive to build a better community to contribute to a better world.

I would like to conclude by chanting Nichiren Daishonin's mantra

Nam Myoho Renge Kyo, Nam Myoho Renge Kyo, Nam Myoho Renge Kyo

Invocation for the Austin City Council Meeting
March 10, 2011

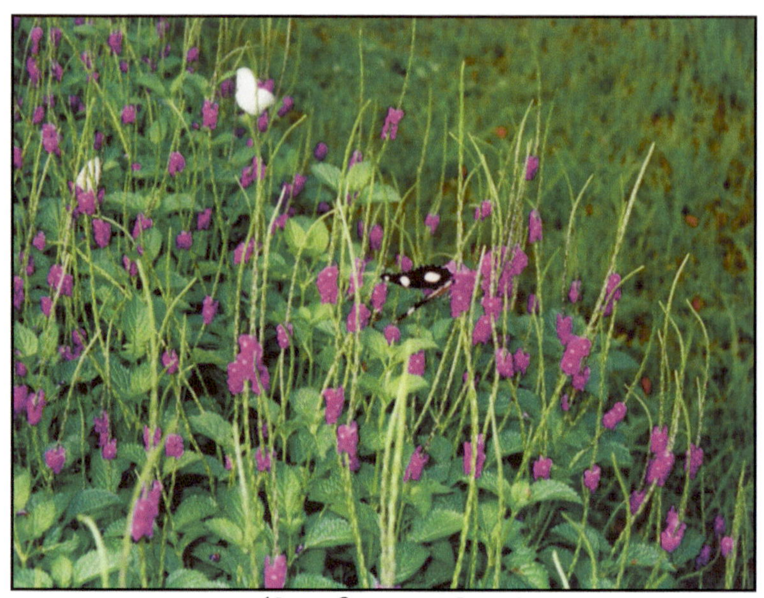

The Nature of Color

Violet, indigo, blue, green, yellow, orange and red
So the spectrum goes
The ingredients making up the palate of infinite color
As the continuous change in wavelength proceeds
From longest to shortest
From red to violet
The luminous energy of radiant beams
Reflecting, refracting
Sending waves of illumination
Producing all the colors of the rainbow

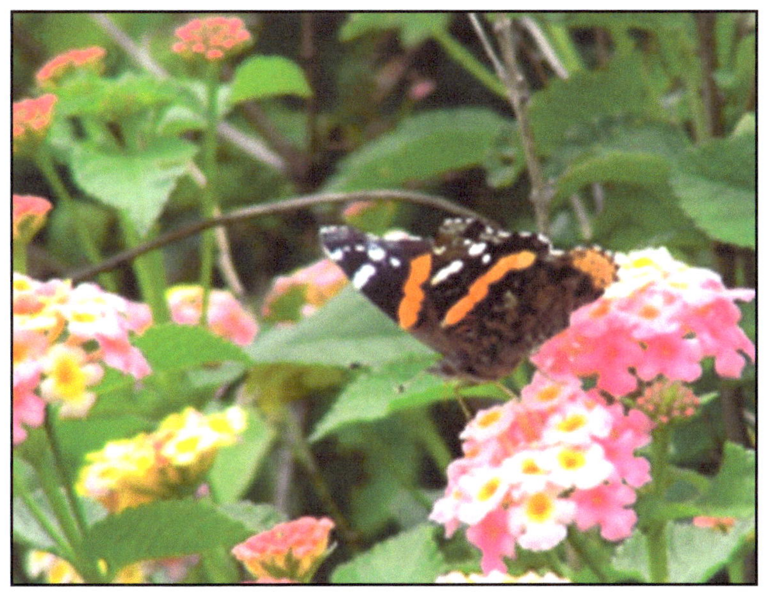

The Color of Nature

Whether lush greens flourishing in the forests
Shades of blue in the seas and skies
The tans of desert sands
The brilliance of snow white peaks
Or the golden glow of fields of grain
Sparkling along the plains
All reflect the vibrant color of nature
Birds and flowers of every hue
Colors of nature pure and true
Appearing in infinite variety
As natural masterpieces
In vibrant living color
Everywhere you look
The color of Nature is
The entire visible spectrum of light

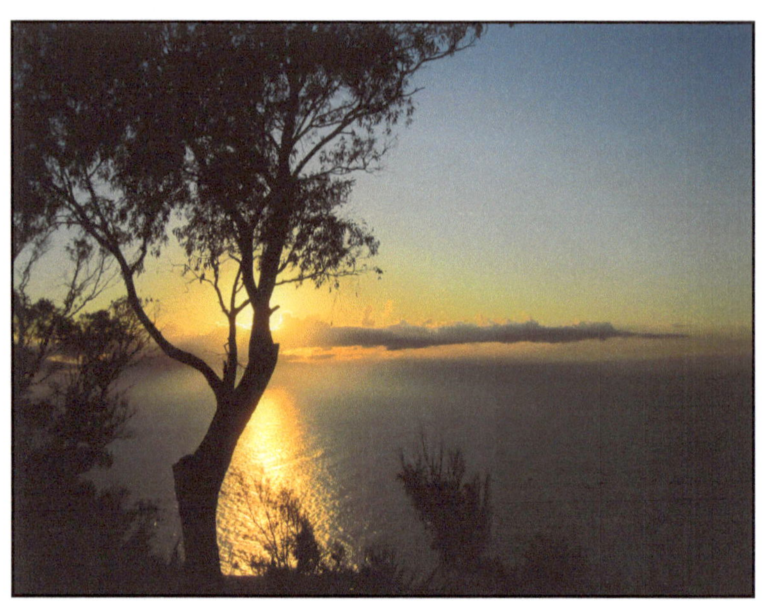

Morning Sun

The morning Sun rises
To awaken all the people of the land
Won't you rise and see the majesty
Of the coming of the dawn
Dawn, hey it's a new day
Sunrise fills the sky with bright rays
It's dawn ... time to rise to life
Get up and hear what I say
It's morning tell everybody
It's dawn ... time to rise to life
Everybody's rising to life
See the people rising to life
It's dawn ... time to rise to life
Won't you rise and see the majesty
Of the coming of the dawn
The time of the morning Sun

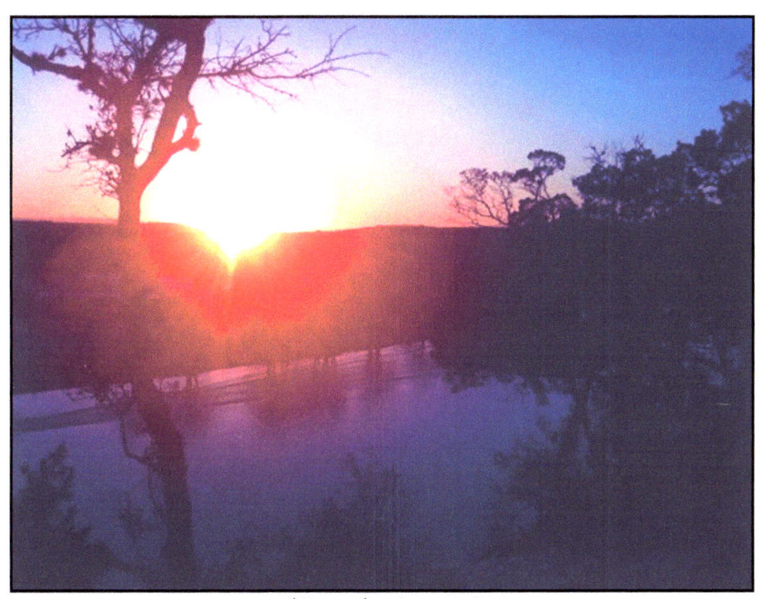

The Today Show

All of My Children
Spend the Days of Our Lives
Searching for Tomorrow
And The Guiding Light
And As the World Turns
The Young and the Restless
Find they've but One Life to Live
And it's on The Today Show

Excerpted from the song "TV Music" by Meredith Beal & Bradie Speller

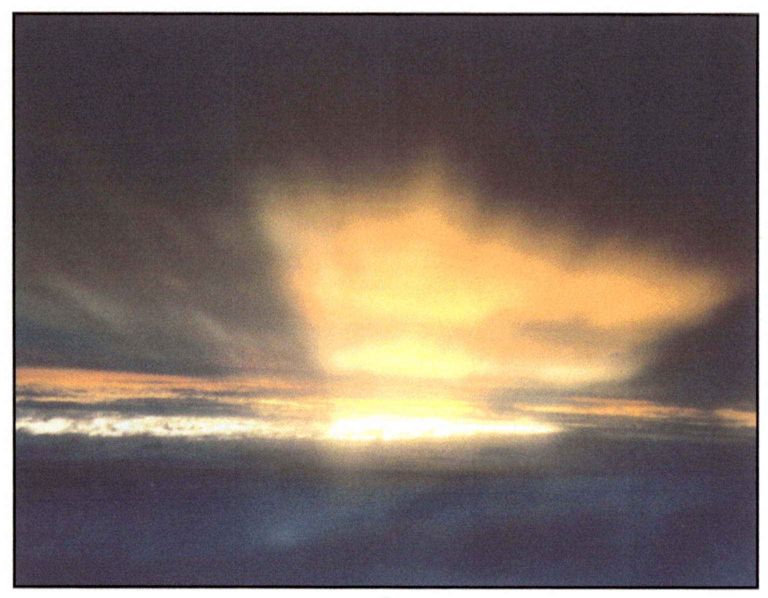

Infinity

Endless movement proceeding forever
Coming from nowhere going everywhere
On and on and on and on
The circle ... the void
The line without beginning or end
All these are like the mind
Touching everything
And touching nothing
Touched yet untouched
The illusive endlessness
Of thought continuing forever
Into infinity

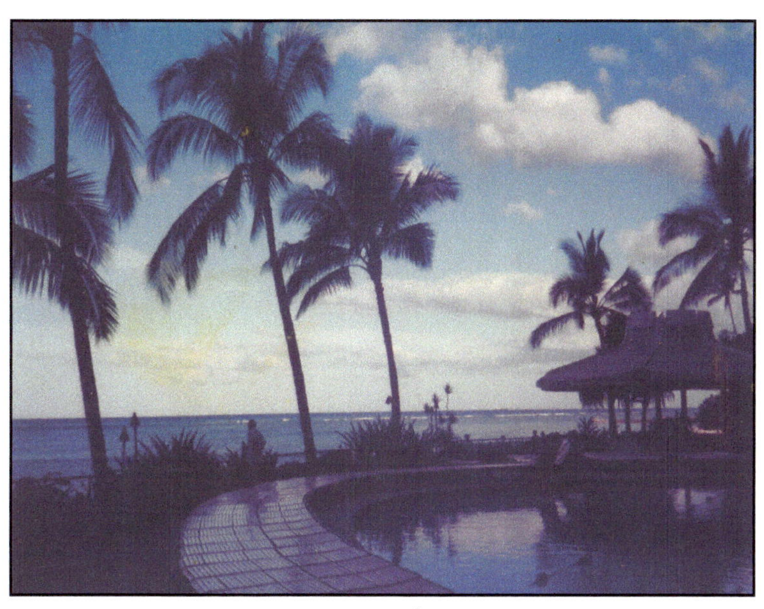

Jamaica

This time has been like a dream — A fantasy in the night
A reverie so real — azure skies and starlight bright
The majesty of sunrise illuminates the land to the call of the morning song
A million shades of blue dance in the ocean
As sunshowers refresh a thirsty Earth
Mountains radiate the lush glory of green while
The Earth basks in the midday Sun
The buzz of life activity fills the air
Birds of myriad colors chatter as they go about their daily chores
While cattle graze leisurely in the fields
Nature's symphony resounds in the night
Melodic harmonies ride the wind, telling the
Noctournal story of the land ... Jamaica
Waves caress the moonlit shore as gentle breezes sweep across the sand
A meteorite dashes across the sky in testimony of the majesty beheld
The sound of night swells with the rapid approach of dawn
Heralding the time to awaken ... from the dream
Time suspended and joy prolonged ... Ah, but alas, the time must come
To awaken from the dream
A dream of beauty and romance in the land
Jamaica

Montego Bay, Jamaica

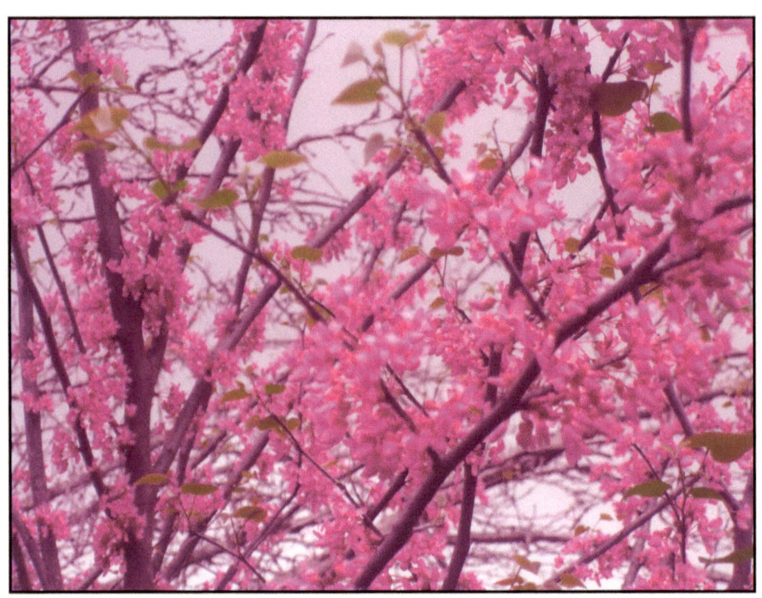

Mission

With joy they go about their daily duty
To share with all their floral beauty
Using every color, tint and hue
Yellow purple red and blue
It is the mission of every flower
To add beauty to the world

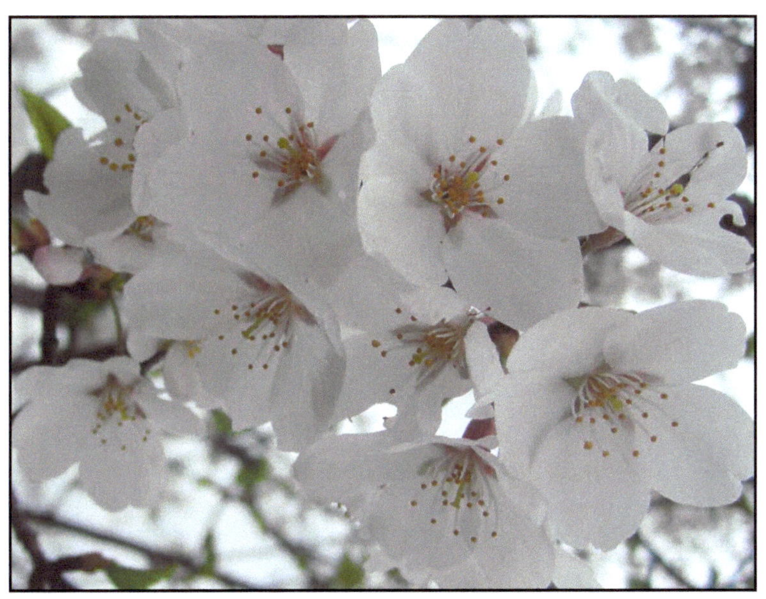

A Day for Joy

Today like every day is a day for joy
To be alive to feel the pulsating energy
And rhythm of life
Is a simple yet profound joy
Often there are so many reasons
Not to see it, not to appreciate it
Preoccupied with the countless
Distractions and diversions
Today like every day is a treasure
Impossible to measure
Earth abound in life
Bursting with living beings
At work ... at play
Today like every day
Is a day for joy

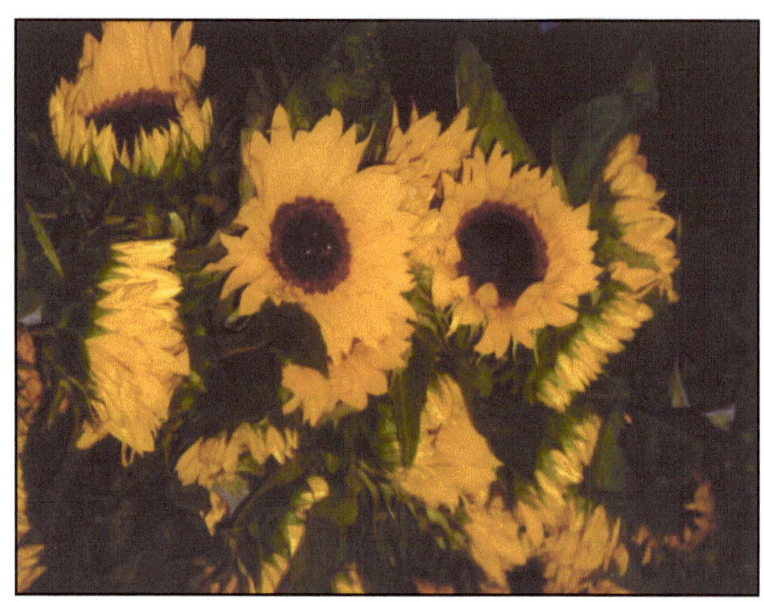

Sunshowers

Sunflowers emersed in sunshowers
Bathing in the warmth of solar rays
Absorbing the energy of the light of day

Sunshowers bestowing radience
On a field of sunflowers
Empowering their grand bright yellow blooms
Like little Suns emerging from the Earth
They brightened the meadow
Spreading cheer in the land
Standing taller than any other flower
They reach to the sky basking in the warmth
Of the Sun

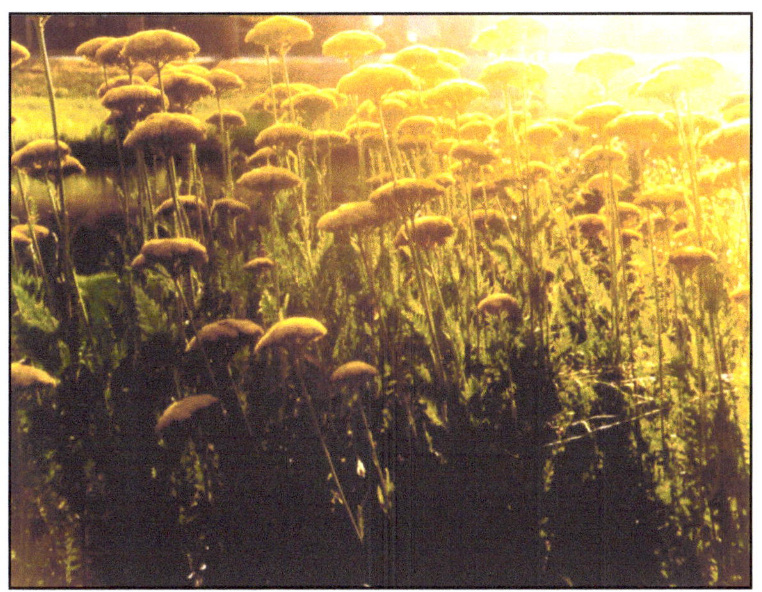

Reaching for the Sun

From the Sun comes the energy animating life
From the Sun comes the warmth longed for
By all the world
From the Sun comes the light sought by
The Green Life
Green consuming light
Digesting the solar meal
To transform its power, energy and love
And deliver it to the remaining earthlings
Filling flowers with solar power
As they reach for the Sun

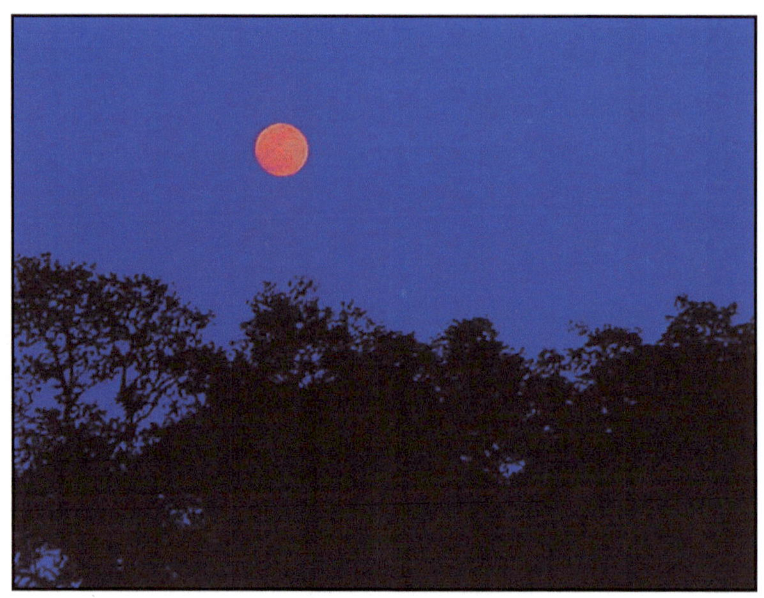

Midnight Dreams

Night falls and moon dust descends upon the Earth
Sprinkling slumber across the land
Ushering us all into the world of dreams
Night time reveries carry me on a journey far
Sailing on the currents of slumber
I travel through the galaxies in noctournal bliss
Midnight dreams
Unlimited by time I freely visit the past and the future
Embedded in the present
Unlimited by space I elatedly visit my family and friends
All over the Universe
Seeking them out wherever they may be
To recall good times and anticipate better days
To work and play with one another
To toil and sweat together
To laugh and cry once again
Midnight dreams
Unlocking the gateway to my deepest desires
Opening the doorway to my deepest dreams
Unlocking the mysteries of yesterday
Envisioning the possibilities of tomorrow

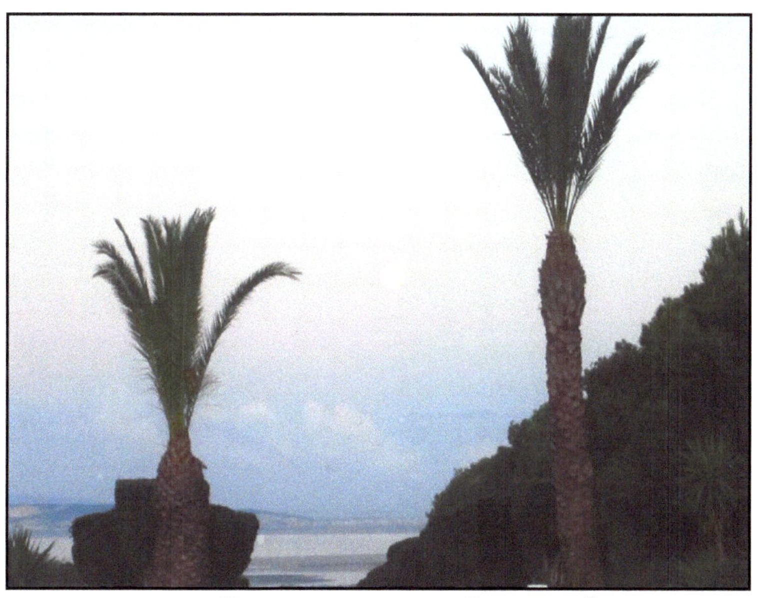

Ode to Mentor and Disciple

Looking back on a time not so long ago when dark clouds hid the light of day
Visions of a sad future dimming hope, obscured the pure true way
Looking back on the time not too long passed when kosen rufu faced its greatest foe
Was a time to come when the pure law was lost and none remained to know?
Could it be that Mappo could come and pass and remain an evil time?
Could those who swore to reveal the jewel not deliver it in time?
Could they not have arrived or worse even yet, arrived and not known the time?
Could they have forgotten their pledge, grown too scared or simply lost their minds?
But who would rise to save the day and restore hope to the land?
Bodhisattva Superior Practices leading the ever victorious band
Bringing music and song and dance and cheer and humanitarian care
The Ode of Mentor and Disciple heard by people everywhere
To those who dwelled the earthlands wide and roamed the people sea
For those who found the gem inside … potentiality
Because of those who arrived just in time to save the day
And all who sought the mystic path and walked the Golden Way
The Law will live and all will have the chance for happiness
And the world will see humanity, live in lasting bliss
Sharing music and song and dance and cheer and humanitarian care
The Ode of Mentor and Disciple heard by people everywhere

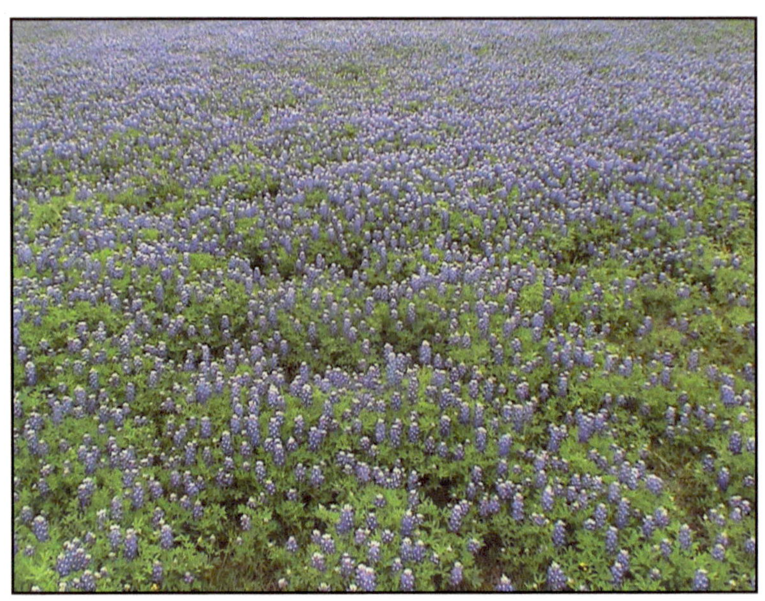

A Spring Meadow

Flowers blooming across the vast meadow
Herald the coming of spring
Bringing refreshment, rejuvenation and awakening
Awakening from the sleep of winter
The phase of hibernation continuing
The unending cycle of life --
Awakening, growth, falling leaves and slumber
White topped bluebonnets appear in the millions
Singing a fresh spring song
With all joining in the harmonious melody of new life
A vibrant chorus of blue reverberating
All across the meadow

Taylor, TX, USA

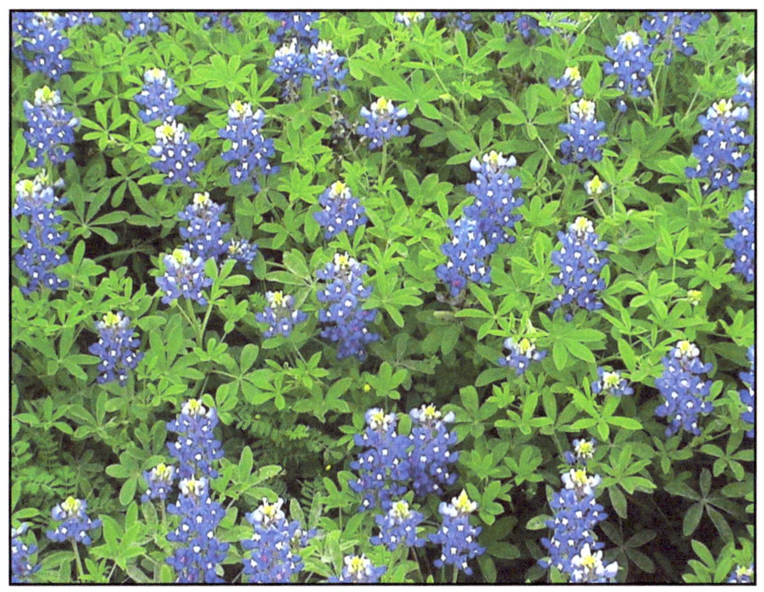

Friendship Seeds

Never can you stop the Sun from shining
Neither can you quench the thirst to know
For the Universe eternally generates new knowledge
The wisdom of which living beings continually strive to know
Seek ye the knowledge of the world and the self
As you leave your footprints in land after land
Your smileprints on face after face
And your friendprints in heart after heart
The noble task of those who seek the golden path
Is like Johnny Appleseed in the Universe
Spreading seeds of kindness far and wide
Which blossom abundantly with the passing of time
Into flowers of friendship
Journey on with your heart full of
Friendship seeds
The world needs now more than ever
Shining beacons radiating the energy of compassion
And reverberating the rhythm of hope
Oh, how admirable the glorious mission of
You who seek the golden path
And walk the Golden Way

Daimoku I Sing

There's a song I sing
A song of joy that wakes the day, oh
I, oh I, sing the morning song

There's a song I sing
A song of peace that greets the setting Sun
I, oh I, sing the evening song

Daimoku I sing, let the joy ring
Let wisdom abound, let the sound resound
True peace within
Let the joy, let the joy ... begin

There's a song I sing
A song of life I sing each day oh
I, oh I, sing the living song

Daimoku I sing, let the joy ring
Build a life so strong, joy will linger on
True peace within
Let the joy, let the joy ... begin

From the song "Daimoku I Sing" by Meredith Clayton Beal

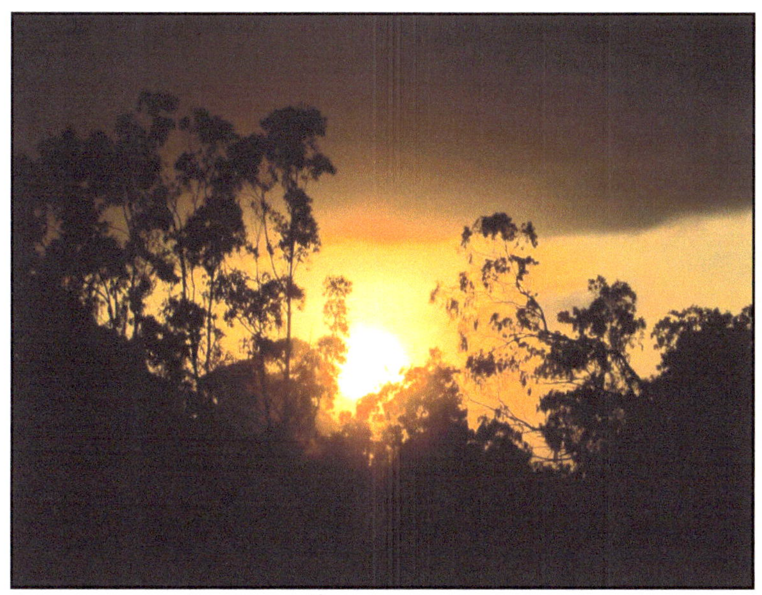

African Sunset

Cooling down from the heat of the day
A day of toil and sweat
Looking forward to an eve of rest
Gazing at a beautiful African sunset
Breathtaking view of a bright horizon ... golden glowing sky
Appreciation of the richness of nature my, oh my, oh my
Days and days of working hard
Incremental progress it seems
Building upon the work of yesterday
Getting closer to my dreams
What is better today because of me
What better future will I see
Will tomorrow's African sunrise
Even brighter be
Venturing from place to place all across the globe
Witnessing uncountable spectacles of beauty
Everywhere I go
No matter where in the world I am
I will never come to forget
The joy I feel whenever I see
The beauty of an African sunset

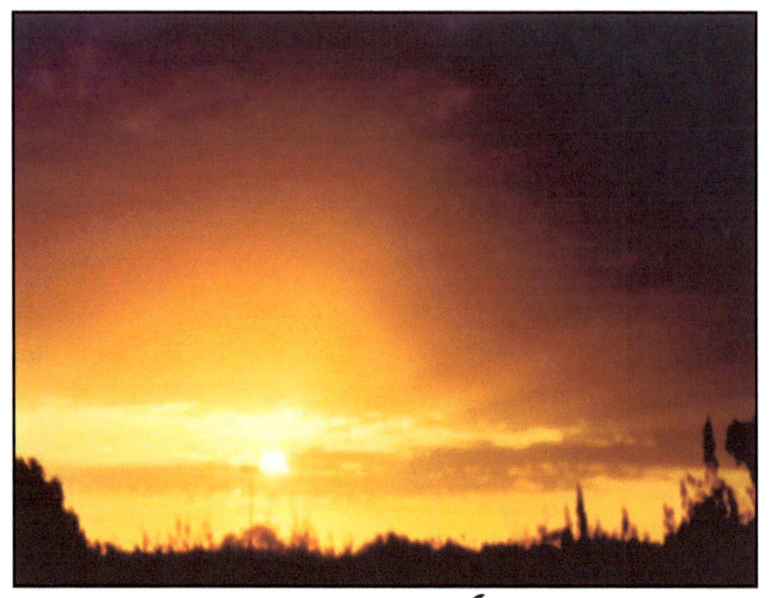

Sunup to Sundown

I woke up in the morning and found that I've lived to see another day
What shall I do today with this gem called life
What good can I do, who can I help, how can I improve
What can I change for the better
What value can I create today that lasts
I venture into the world of daily life meeting scores of people throughout the day
What one good thing can I pass on to them to brighten their day
A word of inspiration ... a word of encouragement ... a word of hope
Whether chance encounter or someone from my daily orbit
How can I treasure each encounter no matter how brief
For it may be the only encounter ... or it may be the last
Planting seeds of friendship all day long ... nurturing those already sowed
What joy is there to see where I am right now
What is it right before me that I must appreciate
Who is it that I must cherish
How can I make the most of my day
I can create, I can share and I can savor
Create, share, savor ... create, share, savor
A cycle of value and appreciation
For a savory taste of life
Moment to moment
Sunup to sundown

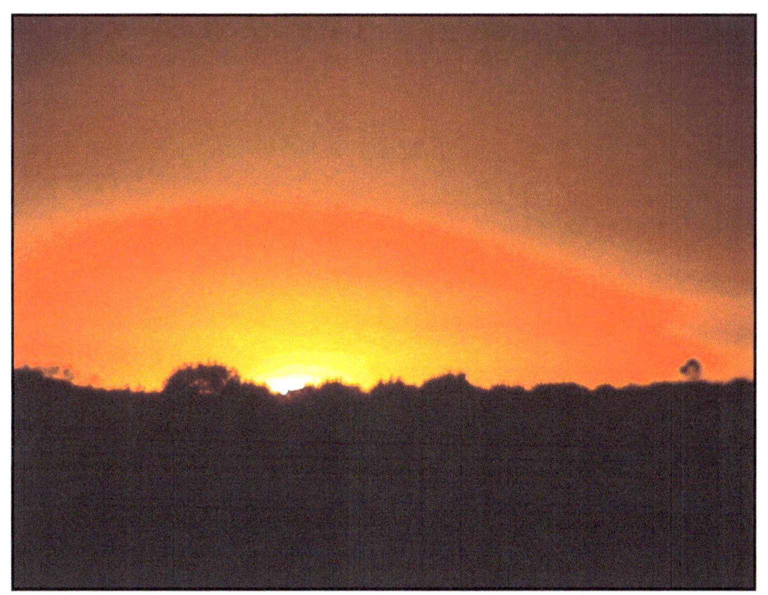

Make a Friend

Make a friend every day
Grow your world of fraternity
Make a friend every day
Every day make a friend

Share your heart every day
Share with the world your humanity
Share your heart every day
Every day share your heart

Every day there's opportunity to make a better reality
Every day we have a chance to change the world
Every day until infinity we can share our joviality
Every day we have a chance to live with joy

Share your mind every day
Share with the world your ingenuity
Share your mind every day
Everyday share your mind

Make a friend every day
Grow your world of fraternity
Make a friend every day
Everyday make a friend

Quotations

It is not the reception of the known
But the process of the seek that is profoundly powerful
For when seek is supreme
No truth can remain unknown.

From "Seek the Light" page 6

The command of abundance thundered throughout the land
And the Earth complied in prolific splendor

From "Abundance" page 12

Make a friend every day
Grow your world of fraternity
Make a friend every day
Every day make a friend

From "Make a Friend " page 67

These are the Golden Days, these are the treasured times
Don't let 'em slip away, cherish the joyful times
These are the Golden Days, these are the precious times
Don't let 'em slip away, treasure the joy.

From the song "The Golden Days" page 47

Can you see harmony in place, see a smile on every face
Hear laughter ever ring, hear humanity all join to sing
Can you see harmony in force,
When everybody taps that everloving source
Feel compassion all around, hear the sound of human joy resound.

From the song "Happiness Yes, Yes, Yes" page 31

Living the dream of profound elation
Secured by daily value creation
Crowned with supreme aprreciation
Three decades living the Golden Way
I celebrate thirty years today.

From "Thirty Years" page 45

All of My Children Spend the Days of Our Lives
Searching for Tomorrow And The Guiding Light
And As the World Turns The Young and the Restless
Find they've but One Life to Live
And it's on The Today Show

From the song "TV Music" page 53

About the Author

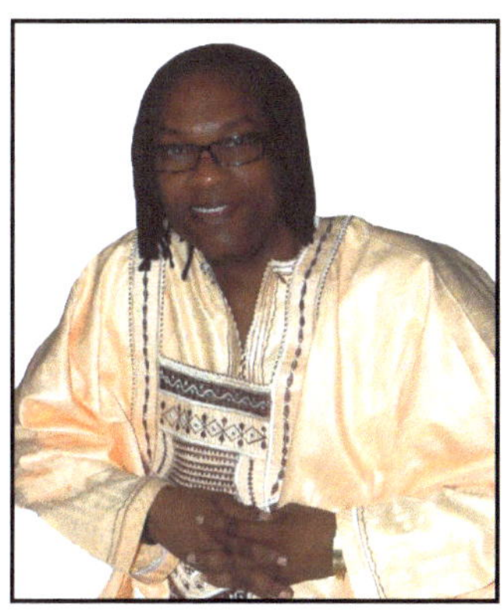

Meredith Clayton Beal

Meredith Clayton Beal is a native of Los Angeles, CA, USA, now living in Nairobi, Kenya. As a global citizen who practices the life philosophy of Nichiren Buddhism, he promotes humanism, peace, culture, innovation and education as he travels around the globe meeting people from all walks of life. The photographs taken during his travels and the poems and song lyrics accompanying them reflect his love of nature, his respect for the beauty in the world and the joy derived from the many treasures the Earth has to offer to those who pay attention. ***Victory Every Day*** *is a story of life, inspiration, appreciation, hope and victory.*

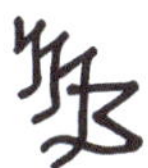

www.ingramcontent.com/pod-product-compliance
Lightning Source LLC
LaVergne TN
LVHW052256100826
845147LV00001B/67

* 9 7 8 0 6 1 5 7 0 7 0 4 4 *